A MILE A DAY

How to get to where you want to go in life,
and stay away from the places you don't.
Reaching one Milestone at a time.

by
Joseph Ligé

Dedication

This book is dedicated to the person who taught me how to live my life to the fullest. It honors the man who showed me how to turn normal everyday life into the life I want to live. My Grandfather, Papa Joe Wiley, encouraged me to follow the path of desire with an unyielding faithful determination in order to reach my dreams.

My Grandfather told me the formula to a fulfilling life is:

Desire + Determination = Achieving Dreams.

He educated me on the Rule of "3D."

Table of Contents

Preface

"A **milestone** (from the Latin *milliarium*) is one of a series of numbered markers placed along a road or boundary at intervals of one mile or, occasionally, parts of a mile. This can be used to reassure travelers that the proper path is being followed, and to indicate either distance traveled or the remaining distance to a destination.".... Wikipedia

"The first step is always the hardest. One by one, inch by inch 'til I reach a foot then I'm off and running. 5280 feet later I'm finally there. I have completed a mile in one day. In less time than it takes to watch a 30 min show on TV, I have reached a mile. A little tired, and aching in a few places, but it kind of feels good? Yes, it does. A mile in one day and it feels good." JL

Introduction

Everyday it's all about the 5w's: the who, the what, the where, the when, and the why. Who am I? What am I doing wrong? Where am I going to be in 5 years, 10, and 20? When will I reach my goals? Why am I not there right now? Thoughts, thoughts, thoughts, that is what we do all day, every day, conscious or unconscious. We are humans and we think all the time. Direction is given to us through thought. We even sometimes think the same thing as others, at the same time. The energy that is created as a result of having similar thoughts is great, and those thoughts become stronger until we can direct that same thought energy onto other people. You are what you think you are. And if you think you are, you are.

Our thoughts are so powerful that they have been proven to move mountains. Literally, mountains. Yes, mountains of people to believe in one thing, to think about the same thing at the same time all across the world. For millions of people to focus their energy in the same direction at the same time is true power. To share in the same thought energy with someone is to link with that person or people on another plane—a spiritual plane, a plane of true energy. A blessing comes when you are prepared to receive it, when your mind and thoughts are prepared to receive the gift. Blessings are intended to be passed through us as thoughts and your thoughts must be aligned with that true purpose of the blessing—the purpose of blessing others. But the hardest thing to do of all is to think. The very same things we do all day, every day. What is hard about it, is training yourself to think thoughts that will help you reach your purpose.

You must learn to direct your thoughts in the direction you want them to be in, so you can receive your blessing. You will never get to where you want until you start to think about it. Until that thought consumes you. Until you are thinking so much about it you can't fall asleep. You close your eyes and there it is again. But that's great because that is what you want. That is what you desire. That desire is what makes most people tick. We all desire things—cars, houses, money, a perfect body—but we don't all have the determination to acquire these things we desire.

That determination is what makes that desire consume us. The greater the determination, the less you can think about other things. A great fighter leaves his environment and relocates to a place where they allow determination to transform desire into a burning desire and where they are totally consumed by this desire. What does this mean? It means that true determination means continually making changes to your circumstances, so that everything that surrounds you increasingly makes your desire burn stronger. After you read the first 9 chapters find today's milestone and start from there. If you miss a day or two, just continue on today's date. Keep reading until you have journeyed to all the milestones one day at a time. Use the reflection questions at the end of each month to help you reach your goals.

Chapter 1

Change your thoughts and you change your path

People say, you are what you eat. Well, it can also be said, you are what you think. You have the power to direct your destiny by directing your thoughts toward the goals you want in life and not the things you don't want. We sometimes contradict the things we are taught and pass these incorrect teachings on to others.

For instance we are told that if we do well in school we will be successful, so all we teach is to be successful in school. Not to learn in school, not to take what you can from it and use it. We just say be successful. And in school terms, this means getting As, being on the honor roll, being at the head of the class. But what are these things really teaching? They are teaching that if you do not do as I say you will not be looked upon favorably. You will not be successful, you will not pass my class, and therefore you will be a failure. But perhaps a child is simply not good at taking tests. Perhaps a child hasn't been exposed yet to the subject that he will thrive in. If he/she were taught to be conscious of the fact that he/she still has so many areas to thrive in, he/she may not shut down at that first bad grade in school—he/she wouldn't see himself as a complete failure. If we change the thought process at the initial teachings then we would all reap the benefits of having conscious thoughts.

Chapter 2

A conscious mind

To be made aware can be the most dangerous thing ever allowed by man. Ignorance is bliss. Why would I want to know that, if I think it, I could make it happen?

This is not about rubbing a magic lamp; it's more about finding the magic bean.
To change your thoughts you must plant the seed that will produce the results you want. You would never plant a mustard seed and expect to get a watermelon, right? So, why plant the seed of negative thoughts and expect to get positive results? You have to know what you want first then find the right seed that will produce it.
Knowing is the key and when the chest of ignorance is unlocked the treasure of acquisition is found. Once we know exactly what we want we can begin to find out how to get it. Examine all angles and all possible known ways of making it

happen and also the unknown. Even if you don't know where to begin, the first step is in knowing where you want to go.

Do you want the car or the money it takes to get the car? The house or the money it takes to get the house? If it is the money, you need to know exactly how much it is you need and desire that amount. But what is money? Money is an opportunity to acquire something you want. Just because you have it does not mean you can get exactly what you want. It just gives you a greater chance. By itself it is nothing more than a piece of paper. We decide what that piece of paper can be traded for every day during the open hours of the stock market. When it closes, the amount that it ended at the previous day maintains till the next opening day.

Do you really want money? Or do you want the money so you can get the items and lifestyle that bring you what you *really* want…happiness?

The true question is more than what do you want. It is, "what will make you happy?" Therefore, desire those things and you will bring those things within reach.

Ok, you may ask, don't I need the money to get the things? Well, kind of. You need to know how to spend the money you have to get the things you want and desire. If you want to become rich, study rich people. If you want to be a great chef, study great chefs.

Of course, it's not as simple as that. You may discover that the thing you really wanted and desired is not what you thought it was cracked up to be. Some say that the indecisive mind is the one that never gets what it really wants.

Think about it. Think about a friend who is constantly complaining about his job, but never looks for a new one. He is indecisive in the sense that, he will not make the decision, "I am going to identify what would make me happier and take action to get that even if it means I am taking a risk."

Instead, the thoughts of these people tend to be that they have no choice but to continue in a job they hate.

Well, who said you have too? No one ever said you have to do anything. We are creatures of thought and free thought is the greatest thing ever beset on man. We can and we do. We make our desires into reality because we have the power of decision to do so.

Think it, believe it, and you truly can achieve it. Every time you are having a negative thought, ask yourself if it's even worth thinking about. If it's making you feel bad, and it's not encouraging you to take any sort of action, then it is a useless thought.

However, sometimes we can't help but think about negative things, right ?

Wrong. You can change your path by changing what you focus on and changing your thoughts. When something terrible happens and you are sad about it, let's say a great loss or death, turn that thought around and make it a positive experience.

Let me tell you right now; when I am gone I don't want people to cry. I want them to celebrate. If everyone thought about the good that was in that person who passed away there would be no room to be sad. Yes we can be sad that we can't see them again, but they become even more present in thought.

You think more about someone when you can't see him or her. Think about it; all we have at the end is thoughts -- what people think about us, and how we thought about them; thoughts of love and thoughts of pain, all but thoughts.

Once you are made aware that you can turn your desires into reality, what desires would you allow yourself to acknowledge? We often ignore and suppress our desires because we think they will never come true, so what is the point?

Now there is no way you can sit around and just say, "I will think about being rich and never leave this chair for the rest of my life and that's it." Or can you? Well maybe you really can. Let's see, if a person decided to do this and let's say film it, I bet nowadays with reality TV shows taking over the media you actually might not be that far off. You see, you can make it happen if given the right tool, and the first step in getting the right tool is knowledge.

Knowing how to think, and how to take that thinking and morph it into the physical equivalent is the prize. But, how much desire do you really have to get to the finish line first, to become number one?

Chapter 3

Failure is a result of bad habit

When you are practicing something, you are training to become better at it. The goal is to become good at what you are practicing. You have the desire to be good at it because your level of desire will drive you to the goal.

But you need to look at the failures that will occur as practice shots. Look at them as, training, lifting weights, running—anything you wish—as long as you know that, in order to become good, you are going to take a few shots that don't go in.

No matter how many shots fail during practice, in the end the goal is reached. You have taken plenty of shots and never said once, "it can't be." You just kept trying, because you knew you could do it.

You will not fail if you don't look at failure as a failure. I know that people for ages have said that you should learn something from every failure and success in life. But what exactly are you telling yourself to learn when you learn from failure?

You learn how to fail. So that is all you can take from it. Learn how to succeed from success not failure. Think about what you did *right* in the shot that failed.

It's the persistence, the desire that won't recognize failure that brings what true riches are, what your true goal is, and the results you want. Think about what the end result is and pursue it until you get it. The thing about persistence is you must do it and do it often—take practice shots—to focus on what you want.

The key to this is to write it down. When you write things down, you see what you are thinking right away. This has been done since the beginning of time. When great artists wanted to make something it always started with a sketch, outline, some sort of guide. This is done so you can see what the end will look like before you start. If the result is not really what you want, you change the guide to get the desired result.

Now, some say it does not matter if you write it with a pen or on a computer, but I say use a pen. It takes a lot more for your brain to make your hand write something than it does for it to strike a key. Thoughts stick better in your mind when you write them down, especially when you will be reading this goal everyday a few times a day. Because you see *your* personal handwriting. You associate the written goal with *yourself.*

Put your goal in a place that you look at every day, no matter what. It could be on your mirror in the bathroom or on a night stand. If you are like most people, it's either your computer or remote control. Put the same hand written goal on both of them. Just use tape and a small piece of paper.

Now that you have done the first 3 steps, let's recap.

Steps

1. Think about what it is that you want. Every aspect of the thing you want. What it feels like and what are the consequence that will come with having what you want. If it's a car, how does it feel to be behind the wheel? How does the steering wheel feel? How does the engine sound when you hit the gas? Think about everything so you really know if you want it.
2. When do you want it? Write down the date you want to reach your goal. When do you plan to satisfy that desire that you have in your heart. Be reasonable when picking a date. You would not buy a house instantly because things take time. Plant a seed and think about when the fruit will be ready to harvest.

3. Write it down! Use an ink pen and don't worry about how it looks as long as you can read it. Write your goals and the time by which you plan on reaching your goal. Now that you have written it down, use your best handwriting and write it down again so that anyone else who sees it can read it. By doing so you state to the world what you plan on achieving and by what self-given deadline.

4. Place it. Put it somewhere you will see it every day. For inspiration, you are going to have to read this thing pretty often so make it convenient for yourself. I would suggest your remote control and computer monitor. If it's a laptop, right below your keyboard. You want to

see it as often as you can so it gets in your mind. By writing it twice and making it legible, you have to put more thought into it because you are spending *that* much more time writing it. The more thought put into it makes it easier for you to remember.

5. Lastly, it's all about reading and believing what you read. Really believing it means you act as if it has already happened. It's kind of like role-playing but you know that the role you are playing is yourself, in the future. Once you see how you will be, then you can make any necessary adjustments to get the results you want, or gain the thing you desire so passionately.

All things that man has accomplished have come first in the form of a dream or vision. Man has had to see it before it was made or happen so you know how to make or create that thing you desire. Dream it first and work out all the kinks before you actually work on getting it. Therefore, when it comes time to get to work, there are no surprises. Dream big because the worst that could happen is your dream becomes a little more fit, a little more refined. You can figure out all the things that you need to do to make that dream turn into a reality. Dream fulfilled.

Chapter 4

Desire

Desire is more than a yearning or wanting. Desire is that thing that is deep down inside of you and won't let you sleep some nights. The feeling you had as a kid of wanting to open Christmas presents that were brought by Santa the night before—*that* is desire. That feeling that is so close to nervousness it is often confused for it. But, never the less, it is that thing that weighs so heavily that there is nothing that will or can stop you from getting it.

The people who you have never heard of, their desire was not big enough. All of these people surely had wants and needs but not a big enough desire to never give up, to never let go of their dreams.

You must have the kind of desire that never allows you to accept a word like *impossible*, and accepts no such reality as *failure*.

Time and time again, people have used desire to conquer enemies. The words "burn your ship" is from that same desire. A whole army would travel to another country on ship and once they arrived they would burn their own ships. They would accept no failure. They would conquer that land or die trying.

It is amazing what people are capable of when they have no retreat, when they are forced with a great desire, and what greater desire than the desire to live. If you can create this same type of desire for the things you want in life then you also will be able to conquer a force whom out numbers you by tenfold.

The person who is a world champion has a strong desire. He doesn't let things he doesn't want affect the main thing he wants.

Desire is that road map to achieving an overall career objective, that vacation you have always wanted to take, and even that wife or husband you have dreamed about for years. And like with any map, we can get confused when trying to understand directions. Sometimes, you'll desire things that don't actually serve your ultimate goal. Sometimes, it will actually only *feel* like you desire something, when you don't. When you feel a desire coming on, ask yourself if achieving it will help you reach your ultimate dream.

The idea is to train yourself to recognize which desires serve your purpose, and which do not. This way, you can save all of our energy for the immediate desires that serve your dream, rather than wasting it on useless ones.
Desire cannot only be confusing; it can also bring with it a feeling of isolation. That will happen when you are in hot

pursuit of your desires. Completely pursuing your desires means making room for that, and that can mean cutting out other smaller but more immediate desires. You desire to go out with friends, but you also desire to put time towards your ultimate goal. If you are truly determined the friends will have to wait. This will happen constantly during your pursuit for your desire, and therein lays the feelings of isolation. So be prepared for that, and know that it is not a negative thing.

If you are prepared for this ahead of time, you can likewise decide ahead of time what sort of sacrifices you plan on making in pursuit of your desire. You can decide what sacrifices *have* to be made. Will it be time, a social life, sweat and hard work, or just money? Whatever it will require, are you willing to give it to achieve your desire?

If you have that strong desire and intense determination, then it won't really matter what it takes because you have already signed the check. Once it's signed the process is already in motion and now you just need to wait till the bank of life cashes it for you. How long will they hold your funds before releasing them? That is different in every case. But that waiting period will make it very apparent how much you *really* want to achieve your dreams.

No one can make you desire, people can only help you satisfy that desire. Desire is something in you already and only you can determine your level of desire. Acquiring the knowledge on how to satisfy it is more than half the battle. The rest is just putting that plan into action with your desire leading the way to the finish line.

Chapter 5

Faith

Once you believe you can achieve then achieving becomes a thing of the past. You don't think of yourself as someone who doesn't have what they want. You think of yourself as someone on their way to having what they want. You have to condition your mind to the point where your belief is so strong that all you can think about are the positive things—like the things that you have done that have furthered you towards your dream—because you know them to be true. When your mind is filled with positive emotions and thoughts it will automatically create the state of mind that we know of as, faith. When you have faith that something will take place positively, then a positive emotion is attached with it. It is something you feel good about because you know for sure that it will occur. The only reason your faith is not considered fact is because it has not happened to you yet. That's why it's still called faith. Faith is that fuel that feeds the impulse of thought and gives it life, power and action.

If you ever want to become successful, rich, or a person of status you have to start with the basic feeling of faith. You have to have faith that your desires will come to be. You have to have faith that what you want is possible. It required a lot of faith for the first mission to make it to the moon. It took more than belief in a shorter route to the Indies to guide Columbus to the new world. It took faith and an intense desire to find a new path. It took faith in the Apollo Rocket that it would get them there and back in one piece. Faith combined with a strong desire makes your dreams come true.

Faith is the only known cure for failure. When you are down and out and don't know where to turn, most turn to faith. A belief that the outcome of your hard work and effort will pay off one day must be rooted in faith. You have to have faith that achieving your goals, or those that feel like downfalls, were actually just steps towards getting what you wanted. You will be rewarded and what you are going through is just a part of life. They were inevitable because, you have to try everything that comes to mind when trying to reach your goals. Some of them won't work, but you have to try the ones that don't work to get to the ones that do.

When you mix strong desire with faith then you have not only the gas, but the car to get you there as well; you were awarded a license because of your age and maturity. Now, it is time to take that road trip to satisfy your burning desire.

Faith changes thought into its spiritual equal. Thought goes from being just rational accumulation of knowledge, but it adds meaning to that knowledge. When you think of the things you have faith about, you begin to think more positively about them—you begin to tell yourself, "This *will* happen. Here are the reasons why." And it is through that faith that all things are possible. If for any reason you don't believe strongly that your desires will be satisfied, then they won't. You see, faith is a very powerful thing and it can work against you if you have faith that what you desire won't happen simply because it has not happened yet. Thoughts attract ones similar to themselves. So if you are constantly thinking that there will be a positive outcome from your action it is more than likely going to be some sort of positive outcome. You have to surround your thoughts with thoughts that are geared toward achieving your burning desire if you want your dreams to come to life. By having faith in the overall accomplishment of your desires, you will set a tone for nothing else but success.

Faith removes all doubt by removing all limitations that are set by discerning minds. You have the power to set your own limits and adjust your own boarders to include or disallow positive and negative influences on your dreams. Have faith in yourself if there is nothing else to have faith in and I'm sure you won't let yourself down.

Chapter 6

Imagination
"I see said the blind man." ...(unknown)

The ability to imagine is the thing that keeps the human spirit alive and pushes us to high points while lifting us from our lowest ones. Since the time and age we were able to plan and think about the future, our imaginations have been at work. When we picked up that crayon and started to color in between the lines we had to imagine what the result would be first. That is the reason we chose certain colors and put them in certain places. Now the result might not have been as we imagined but the thought was definitely there. That thought is the starting point of every success. And every success is filled with creative imagination. The most famous inventions or entertainment products were created from the inspiration of someone's imagination and thoughts. And I would argue that imagination is the single most important gift given to man. It is the reason we have achieved the things we have and traversed the time and space in our past. It is the single most important reason why some people make it to the levels they do and see the realization of their dreams. If you can't see yourself there then how could you ever know if you got there or not? Seeing it just requires the use of your third eye; your mind.

People possess the power to see things as we want them to be seen. We imagine what will happen if certain situations come to be, make adjustments and produce the desired result, and if it still does not work then we make more adjustments after we imagine what the new outcome will be.

People that fail to use this power, which has only been awarded to the human race, fail in the aspiration that they set forth in life. Your imagination just needs to be exercised more often, to get it in the proper shape it needs to be in to focus on your desires, so you can reach your dreams.

Imagination is the reason we even have dreams in the first place. What would be the benefit in having a dream if we couldn't even think about what it would be like to have that dream reached? Why would we be given the same emotions and opportunities as everyone else if we could not see them attained? Imagination is something that levels the playing field, which all of us starts on, and is the greatest equalizer amongst all people. Essentially, if we all begin with imagination we all have the same power. You can control what a man does but there is no way to control the reach of one's imagination. Seeing oneself as the person they want to be is the driving force behind all great things that have been accomplished. We only do things because we can imagine the possible outcomes of our actions.

In life we are constantly judged by our reaction time to what we imagine. The slower the reaction time, in most cases, the slower we achieve our objectives. You can't hit a baseball if you can't see what will happen before you swing the bat. If a person could not train the third eye to see what the outcome of the swing would be, the hallways in Cooperstown would be empty. Failure to train will result in failure to reach goals. Failure, is only reached by those who fail to imagine.

Chapter 7

Determination

It's up to you to decide on what will prevent you from ever attaining your dreams. You must have an unyielding determination to get what you want. The same kind of determination basketball players have when they go up for a dunk. Nothing will stop them from getting to the rim. Now, it might not be easy and you may have to go over, around or even though another player but you have the determination to get there.

We are all born with the ability to do almost anything that we can think up. But what separates us is the determination factor. What are you willing to sacrifice to get what you want, how much are you willing to go through pain, misery, and most important time to get the things you want out of life? Well as they say, *if it was easy then everybody would do it.* There is nothing given to anybody in life who does not have to sacrifice something in return for it. The most well-known sacrifice was the one of Jesus Christ who sacrificed his life for others. That is the ultimate definition of love: sacrifice. You can tell how much you love someone or thing by how much you are willing to sacrifice for that person or thing. Are you willing to give your life? Are you willing to give your time? The level of sacrifice will yield its deserving result.

When you combine this type of determination with desire you can reach your dreams. The only way you can lift more weight than you ever have, or run the furthest you ever have, is by having the determination to do so. You have to get to that point and getting there is never easy. The only thing that can make you get up and go to the gym is the level of determination you have to get to that mile marker, and to get in that bench press club. No one can give you energy; you have to earn it by training your muscles and lungs to handle the workload it requires to get to your goal.

Having the determination to stand by a desire means understanding yourself, the laws of nature and true happiness. When you understand these, you will know *why* you are determined, and *how* you will complete your goal. You have to at some point determine that you are here to do something and once you know what that something is, create the sense of determination that won't take no for an answer.

If you want a job in some sort of company, you can get it if you don't let anything get in your way. If you do the proper research and take the necessary steps to get the job, in all likelihood it will be offered to you. That may require certain things like going to the right schools or having the proper credentials to even be considered, but the sooner you know what you want, the sooner you can start the mission to get there. Plant that magic bean and grow a stock to climb to the top of.

Determination is the thing that won't let you sleep at night. Determination is the reason we break records. Without determination there would be no success because we would have no idea when we got there. We would not know what we were working for, so we would not work. If someone offered you a job and did not tell you what you were going to get paid, you would probably not take the job. There has to be a reason to work, an end to a means, or it would not be called work. It would just be a service you were doing and didn't know why you were doing it.

Much like a robot that just does something because it is programmed to do it. There is no reward for the robot doing a good job; the robot cannot feel, so it just does. We are not robots, and because of that we can do things that we want to do if we are determined to do so.

Chapter 8

DREAMS
"To dream is to live and to live is to Dream"

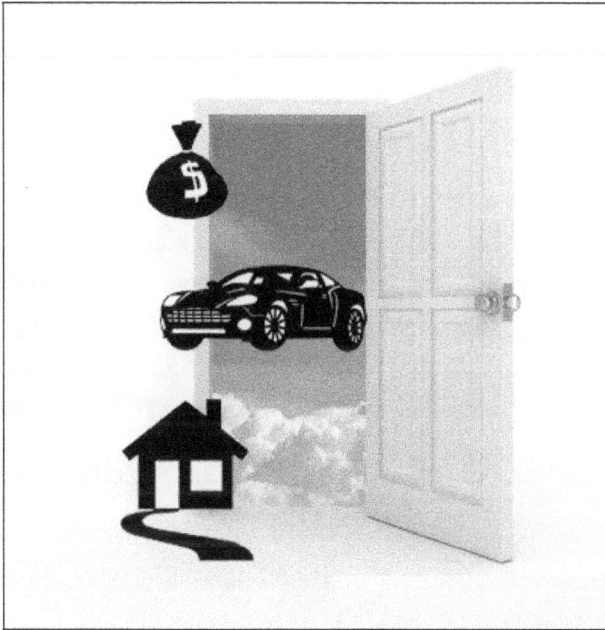

Dreams are the reason we make plans. It is through dreams that we create steps and follow them 'til we reach where we want to be. The reason we have desire is because we have dreams. But dreams are just thoughts 'til we put legs on them to give them motion and life.

There are two different kinds of dreams. The dreams we have every night or most nights. Sometimes, when these are bad, they are called nightmares. The other kind of dream is the one we have for things we want in life, places we want to see and the kind of person we want to become. If we focus on the dreams that we create then we set ourselves up for attaining goals.

When you complete a goal you become closer to accomplishing your dreams. There is no time like the present to start believing that it is possible to reach these dreams you have. No one can tell you what to think and when, so you can focus most of your time thinking about how you can accomplish your dreams. That's when your dreams manifest themselves into reality.

Dream big because if you shoot for the stars falling short only means you land on a cloud. The higher you aim, the greater your desire and determination have to be in order for you to reach your desired result. You have to put more into it if you want a lot out of it. It is not a complex formula at all. It is just based on the laws of nature. To achieve more, you must give more.

You don't necessarily have to work harder, but rather smarter. Use your time well and most effectively to reach where you want to be in life. Focus your sights on the dream and work towards your goals each and every day. By working towards these goals you give purpose to life and meaning to your existence. Most people don't know why they are here. They do a job every day, but besides paying their bills, they don't know why they do it. They know *that* job is not the reason they are here, but they don't know what that reason is. The answer lies within their dreams. The answer is we are here to fulfill our dreams. And the only way to do it is follow the right formula, using the right ingredients.

It may take several things to reach a dream and make it reality, but when you're there it will be all worth it. If you really want happiness then you must do the thing that will help you accomplish your goal. You may not enjoy those exact steps, but they will make you happy because you know why you're doing them.

It is said that too much of anything is not good for you, but I am here to say you can't dream too much. As a matter of fact most people don't dream enough and those are the ones you probably have never heard of. The people who do reach their dreams end up finding ways to help others also reach theirs. You give to receive, and receive to give more.

Chapter 9

Persistence
"Never give up, and never give in…..."

You got to keep climbing if you plan on reaching the top. You have to have the determination to make it and the persistence to keep going no matter what. You have to stay on top of it or it will stay on top of you. You can make your dreams come true if you are persistent about the work it is going to take to get there. Lacking of this necessary trait is one of the fastest ways to failure. Some people want things in life, even have a burning desire to attain them and are determined to do so, but they don't do the things it takes to get there. You not only have to start but you have to make sure you follow through and have the faith in what you are doing.

There are a lot of great thoughts but few are ever made into reality because of fear of criticism. People are not willing to put up with what others will say, so they never reach the planning and action stage. They lack persistence.

The great thing about persistence is that it is a state of mind that you put yourself in, so you can build upon it or take from it. This is something that is entirely up to you. Once you have a dream in mind, and have given yourself reason to pursue that dream, difficulty will never surmount you. You will come across it, but it will not defeat you. You will be victorious if you have the persistence to keep working till you are there.

Building on your persistence requires working with other people, because you can't do it alone. You have to cooperate with the rest of the world in order for the world and all that's in it to cooperate with you. Therefore, you must examine what your habits are and make the necessary changes to align them with your dream. Your habits are the direct indicator of how persistent you are. If you are on your way to a few goals that you have set, then you are doing things every day to help you get there.

Persistence builds the road that you will travel on your way to your dreams. Allow your persistence to get you through the rough weather, and allow your determination to help you reach your dreams.

It's not difficult, it just requires you to really desire your dreams and follow through with persistence until your determination pays off. Rely on your ability to carry out your plans. Your plans will also help encourage the persistence you need to get what you really desire, because each time you follow through with just one of your plans you have more faith in yourself.

Make sure you are certain of what it is you want because another fast killer of persistence is guessing instead of knowing what it is that you desire. You cannot have faith in gaining something if you don't know what it is you are putting your faith in. So know your plan and have persistence to carry out that plan until your objectives have been met. By doing this you will have created not only a better quality of life but also given purpose to what you are doing.

January

January 1

It's better to spend time loving the one you're with than just being with the one you love. Love is something that requires action to continue to grow. Love is a combination of chemistry and *the things you do* to keep it alive. If you spend your time just *being* with the person you love then, one day, that person may end up loving someone else. Spend time showing love. It's an investment with a good return. If you're not sure if the one you're spending your time loving is worth the investment, do like you would do with any investment; look at the market and compare your investment to the standard return for its type. If it's below market return, then it's a bad investment. And that will hurt. You will be frustrated that your investment yielded no return. But, with any risky investment, be prepared to lose as big as you might win…(3D)

January 2

Just as water washes away dirt, our past is washed away with the present. You have the opportunity to live right now the way you want to. And remember, all of the time you will be granted in life, you are spending some of it *every second.* Many people subconsciously believe they are *waiting* for their life to begin. It has already begun. If you feel like you are waiting, that simply means you aren't making the best of it. Squander your time and you will squander your life. It's not about what you have in your pocket that ultimately makes you a joyful person. It's about that thing in your chest we call a heart. How much of it you share with others and how much of it you allow others to fill. Wash away all bad things in the past with joyful times in the present. Create those times. Accept those times. Don't run from them for fear that they will turn out the same way as the past did….(3D)

January 3

The standards you set for yourself should always be higher than the ones other people set for you. You should demand more from yourself than others do because they don't know what you are capable of. They don't know how much potential you have. They can only make a judgment based on what they see. And you might be hiding your potential because you are afraid for people to ask *more* of you. As a result, the expectations of others are always lower than your abilities. If you strive for more than what is sufficient for others, you'll always get more than what they expected to reward you with…(3D)

January 4

Just as sailors used to follow the stars to reach their destination when they were engulfed by the darkness of the sea, you should follow the stars in your life that are bright and shine through the deepest and darkest nights. These are the people you look up to. The term "role model" comes from the concept that these people are in the role you would like to be in one day. The greatest thing about wanting to walk in the same footsteps as another is the path is already made. A map has been drawn and you can see where and when the road became more challenging. You can prepare yourself for those times. When you finally realize your dream, turn around and see who is now following in your footsteps. Be the guiding light to success and darkness will always move from your path....(3D)

January 5

We use tires that are round because they move smoothly with less friction. Sharp edges slow us down. When you are trying to move forward in life, approach the journey with rounded edges. If possible, approach it with none at all. Remove all the sharp edges in your life that are causing friction and preventing you from enjoying a smooth ride. If you want to reach your destination with the greatest ease, make sure your tires are in good condition and filled with the right amount of air...Make sure you are stable and energized....(3D)

January 6

All mountains and challenges are the same; they look easy to conquer from afar, but as you get closer to the starting point they seem more difficult. The easiest moment is when you think about being on top of the mountain. Then, with that in mind, you go to the base and start the climb. Remember, to complete any challenge you must take the first step. Do not be intimidated by the million steps to come. Many start the race but few cross the finish line or see the world from the view at the top because they are intimidated by the steps to get there, and they do not give themselves credit for taking the first step...(3D)

January 7

Every time you assume you know everything about anything you are met with some form of challenge to your expectations. Never think you know everything. Simply strive to know enough. Enough means knowing what you need in order to get what you want out of a situation. No matter if you know *everything* about that situation. Useless knowledge is the same as no knowledge at all about something. If you spend more time learning how to reach your desires you won't have time or room in your day to take in useless information. More importantly, you will learn how to filter out useless information…(3D)

January 8

Differences can bind us together or push us apart. Which will it be depends on how much we open our hearts and accept things that are different from ourselves. If instead of being jealous of what someone else has or is, embrace it and strive to understand and appreciate it. When you do this, the difference will bind you and that person like opposite ends of a magnet. But if we place judgment on them because of the differences then we will drift apart. We will become afraid of their differences because we do not understand them. The more we learn about others differences the more alike we discover we truly are…(3D)

January 9

It's said home is where the heart is. Since your heart is in your chest, then you must take care of your body. You must feel comfortable in your own skin—that is where the feeling of home comes from. When you need comfort—when you need to feel at home—find it within by knowing yourself better. You can lay your head on any pillow and fall asleep but you can't call any place home. It takes love to make a home. But once you love yourself, you can feel at home almost anywhere….(3D)

January 10

Just as the shortest distance between two points is a straight line so is the quickest way to your goals. If you take detours and get side tracked it will only slow you down. But if you stay straight and don't let anything knock you off course, then your goal will become a reality. The trick is to learn how to recognize a detour and differentiate it from the straight path. Once you learn this, reaching any goal will be second nature. Get used to being successful so success can find you more often. Do not brag about your successes, but let the happiness of them show on you. You can always spot success in a room full of failures by looking for the ones with the biggest smile…(3D)

January 11

If you never find something that you love doing then everything will have the same appeal and attraction—nothing will stand out. If you have no focus, then you will never know if you hit the target. You can't depend on luck to bring you satisfaction because you will spend an eternity waiting. You have to make your own luck by working as hard as you can to accomplish your goals. You will be rewarded not only with your goals but you will also become mentally in shape to receive them when they come…(3D)

January 12

Most people who end up with the wrong crowd are usually insecure. When you are insecure with yourself, you constantly worry that you are not doing or saying the right thing. You are not even the *right person*. This is a personality trait that some people will take advantage of—typically, other insecure people. They make you feel as if they care you about when no one else seems too. But the truth is no one can care for you like you can. No amount of love or care from another person will come close to the feeling of love for yourself and when you have that love for yourself, you become far more selective of whom you allow into your life. You become more aware of who truly cares about you, because you can compare the feelings of caring you receive from them to the ones you have for yourself...(3D)

January 13

You never really know how the impact that a "hello," or "how are you" can have on someone's day until you're on the receiving end. Some call that southern hospitality but I like to call it a day brightener. Day brighteners are simple words and gestures like opening the door for someone, or letting a person with only a few items go ahead of you in the grocery store. The more people you can make smile in a day, the more pleasant of a person you will become...(3D)

January 14

Add a prefix and a suffix to your life. Add meaning to what was before you, by making something better out of it. Make proud those that came before you, by furthering their work. Do things in your daily life that cause your ancestors to smile on you and feel proud of the person that preceded them. Make them feel that what they did matters, by making the best of it. This is how you add a prefix to your life. Leave something behind for all future generations by fulfilling your destiny. Bring opportunity to those that might not have had a chance if it were not for you. This is how you add a suffix. Focus on the now and allow your suffix to be given to your name after you are gone. What you did while you were here will make that suffix very clear. But for now, be in the now. ...(3D)

January 15

Spend your time trying to be upwind and not downwind. Be the one adding to people's lives and energizing them, rather than taking from them and draining them. If you spend your time doing good things for others, more and more opportunity will open up for you and you will have a choice of what you receive and when. You will suddenly have hundreds of people who keep you in mind and think of kind things to do for you. But, if you are someone who just takes, your only option is to take what that person has at that time. Beggars can't be choosers, and neither can takers....(3D)

January 16

Just as there are warning lights at every train crossing, there are warning lights in life at every decision we make. This is called our conscious. It's up to us to decide if we want to pay attention to these warning lights or not. Most who have been hit by a train though the warning lights were further away. And, any time something in life goes terribly wrong it's because we thought that the consequences were not a reality—that they were a far off, vague concept. Pay attention to warning signs. Even though they can feel like it at times, their purpose is not to slow us down, but to keep us from getting hurt….(3D)

January 17

The only thing you need to feel like a star is to shine to the ones who encounter you every day. You don't need to be a celebrity. You don't need to do something phenomenal. You can brighten someone's day simply by being better than they expected you—or humanity—to be. If you live with the intent of putting smiles on faces, then your desire to satisfy will be met with a deep sense of joy because you can reach that goal daily. Simply by sharing your warm hearts with others, do you make their cold hearts warm…(3D)

January 18

Seeking recognition from others will rarely lead to genuine satisfaction. You should always strive to satisfy your inner desire for the particular thing that will make you feel successful. You will be rewarded with the proper recognition when it is due. But if it never comes, simply knowing you did what you set out to do will be enough. What is done in the darkness will soon be brought to the light. Just keep doing what you feel is right and your reward will be greater than all the gold or fame on earth….(3D)

January 19

Every time you want to complain because your life is not where you want it to be, take a mental picture of where you *do* want it to be. Keep that picture in focus constantly. Concentrate on it on the days when all you can think about is your discontent with the current state of things. Make your goals worth all the effort you are putting in to reach them. Don't just focus on graduating. After you do, you won't know what to do with that piece of paper you worked so hard to get. Focus on a career as your goal, so that you will pay closer attention to the skills your learn in school and actually make a plan for how to use them...(3D)

January 20

You are truly the captain of your ship and responsible for all the people you allow to go on the journey with you. You may have a navigator but the direction of when you go and what direction you go is ultimately up to you. Your decisions affect the outcome of your entire crew and determine the destination you will arrive at. You also have no other choice but to go down with your ship if it sinks. That is the protocol—the captain always must go down with his ship. All the crew you have assembled will abandon you and float away on life rafts while you sink. So make sure you pick your crew wisely. Surround yourself during your voyage with those who will speak highly of you after your ship sail is seen for the last time above water...(3D)

January 21

It is said that a quitter never wins but there is also value in knowing when it is time to stop. Knowing the difference giving up and stopping something that is not right for you will help you avoid unnecessary turmoil and help you make better use of the limited time you have. Knowing when it's time to leave a situation is the key factor that some of the greatest success stories have mastered. Most people who make it to great heights came from a less fortunate place. They made it to great heights because they knew when it was time to leave that place. Not all battles are worth fighting and not all races are worth finishing…(3D)

January 22

Sometimes the smallest thing that is over looked can impact a life. Even a blade of grass can change the path of an ant if it gets in its way. Don't let the little things in life turn into large roadblocks. Instead, use them to boost you up so you can reach a place that may seem too high…Overcome them, and you will automatically be closer to your goal…(3D)

January 23

Just as leaves on a tree turn brown and fall to the ground, your pain will shed with the coming season. If you don't like the way you feel right now, you can do something about it or wait it out. Nothing lasts forever and time will forever change the face of all living and non-living things. All you have to do is look at the difference a day makes and you will soon realize how precious the time is we have. We must use it to impact the world around us. Don't allow anything or any person to change what you plan to become or want to be. That will only be a waste of time because ultimately only *you* can know what you really want to be. Even if you follow someone else's lead for a little, you will always realize you were meant to go on your own path. And time spent following someone else will have been a waste…(3D)

January 24

By changing the way you appear to others you change the way you feel about yourself. The better you present yourself to others, the more they will complement you on how well you look. The more people complement you, the more self-esteem you will have. When the time comes that you are alone and can't depend on them to complement you, you can always use your memory to remind yourself of their complements. When the compliments stop and no one says anything, look in the mirror and complement yourself. There is no bigger motivator than yourself and you should always be your biggest fan. If you are, there will always be others willing to hop on your band wagon…(3D)

January 25

To find peace you must fight through all conflicts. After all battles, there is a time of rest and a time for peace. There is always an end just as there was a beginning and they both come with the same state of mind: mental and physical rest to prepare for your next struggle. There will never be a time when everyone or thing agrees on everything. There would never be growth if there were nothing to compete with or against. You need there to be opposites because too much of the same thing is never good…This is why countries constantly change leadership…A leader with opposite ideas must always step in to re-balance the state of things…(3D)

January 26

The best way to celebrate a victory is by setting another goal and start working toward it right away. Celebrate victory with another victory. Use the momentum to go and get yourself another win. It is said that bad things come in groups; your victories can come in groups as well if you keep the same attitude and focus you had when pursuing your first goal. Win often to succeed daily. Success is the result of many small battles that lead to ultimate victory...(3D)

January 27

Don't rush things that you want because only sloppy results will come. Most things that are rushed are not completely ready to be used when you finish them A cake that is taken out of the oven before it's done cannot be called a cake because it's still just dough. Relationships are the same way. Taking your relationship to the next level before its time will never result in a long lasting relationship and will usually fail quickly...(3D)

January 28

When things in life are not going the way you want—a job is not paying enough or the weather is bad—find a place within that brings you internal peace. Learn what causes you to relax and makes your muscles less tense. Focus on things that have been proven to bring you joy and happiness. Relive those experiences through memory. That is why we have memories—to pull up emotions of past events....(3D)

January 29

Pressure is something that can come in many different forms and if not handled properly can cause its container to burst. When you are faced with a lot of pressure, use it to transform yourself into a diamond. Find a release valve in your life so it does not build up.

You possess the power to change the amount of pressure by changing your environment or situation....(3D)

January 30

It is said a rich man is judged with a heavier hand then a poor one and that is because a rich man has more tools to transform his life. A poor man lives life and accepts what he is dealt, but a wealthy man looks at what he has been dealt and trades his cards in for what he wants. You will never reach the goals your heart desires if you just accept life for what it is. There is a huge difference between living life and making life what you want it to be. As far as we know, you only have this lifetime to make an impact. Don't waste your time because you never know when your time will expire...(3D)

January 31

Never take for granted the smallest thing someone may do for you even if they did not know they were helping you. When something is causing your day or week to be bad, look at all the little things that are happening around you that can help you appreciate life just a little bit more. You have all the time you are given right now to live a happier more joyful life and it all starts with appreciation. All of the riches in the world would do you no good if you did not appreciate them. Most people go through life not ever thinking about all the other people who have impacted their lives positively...(3D)

Questions

1. What impact on the world do you want to have?

2. What needs to change in order to have greater satisfaction in your everyday life?

3. What do you want to be, do and have?

February

February 1

The one sure way to maintain a healthy and productive life is to make sure you have consistent goals that you are trying to reach and have established steps with which you can measure your progression. Some goals you might never reach, but the simple fact that you made progression toward them will help you when you are pursuing other goals. When you get in the habit of taking steps toward your goals then your successes will come frequently. Make note of the process rather than the results so you can reuse that process when you have new desires…(3D)

February 2

If you spend your time worrying about what other people think then you will never have time to enjoy who you are. Your own opinion of yourself is far more important than what others think of you, because when you close your eyes they are not in front of you. You are the one who must deal with yourself constantly. There is no way to stop people from thinking what they want but you can stop how much you choose to listen to them and in turn what you let affect you…(3D)

February 3

Achievement is recognized whether the acts are good or bad. The only difference between the accomplishments of a great thief and a great poet is how they went about reaching their fame. Opportunities to become an individual of importance present themselves quite often, but often people cannot make the decision to take them. We all have dreams of being great but few are willing to do what it takes to get such a title. This is because taking the opportunity to be great is something barely anyone else is doing, so it seems frightening or feels isolating...(3D)

February 4

The ones who go through the most are the ones who are best prepared to receive the rewards that are in store for them in the future, the reason being that they know the full value of the reward because they worked for it. There is a large percent of people who win the lottery and end up broke a few short years later. Essentially, they were rewarded for something they were not prepared for. They were given more than they had ever had and did not know what great responsibility came with it. There is no way to prepare for the unknown in life but if you prepare for the future you want, when that future becomes the present you will be ready to receive it...(3D)

February 5

When you are pointed at as the result of something that has gone wrong you must look at the person who is doing the pointing. Most of the time the one who is pointing is being pointed at too and wants to pass the feeling they feel onto others. Stop the cycle. Don't point a finger. Strive to become the person who corrects the problem not the one who points it out. The ability to correct a flaw is a much greater skill than the ability to identify one....(3D)

February 6

The most difficult thing is to let go of something you love. To give up something to someone else is to sacrifice...and to sacrifice is to love. Sacrifice is the purest form of love and the greater sacrifice the greater the intensity of love you display. When you give often, you receive often. That's because of the energy you are putting out into the world. The more love you spread in the world the more love the world will show and give you in return. That love is out there because *you* put it out there. Everything we do has an effect on the rest of the universe. Some things are more direct and easier to observe than others, but never the less they do have effects...(3D)

February 7

We judge others by the way they treat other people. When you see someone help another person, it shows that they have a caring heart and are willing to put others first. Not many people will stop an offer to help if you are on the side of the road with a flat tire. Even fewer would think that the one who does stop has pure intentions and isn't just trying to get something from the person with the flat tire. You can't expect someone else to stop and help you if you are not willing to stop and help someone else...(3D)

February 8

It takes a great deal of sacrifice to deal with someone else's flaws. Overcoming these flaws—learning to love someone with their flaws—is the ultimate test of a relationship. If you pass that test, you get the strength required to get through the roughest of times. If you believe that all the effort is worth the results, then that positive attitude will persist when you are faced with further negative situations. You have seen that that attitude got you the results you wanted the first time, so you will uphold it again and again. You have to allow your intentions to guide your way as you journey toward your goals...(3D)

February 9

 Relationships seem to become more difficult the closer they get to commitment and that is because commitment is not a natural thing. This is why in order for people to marry they must feel the strongest bond—love. Love is the super glue that can keep people together forever through the good and bad. The only problem comes when both people don't share in this same feeling. The glue is still present but one person is glued to a ticking time bomb that will only cause frustration and end in destruction and pain...(3D)

February 10

Some people never understand the importance of helping a person in need until they are in need themselves. They wait until something happens to them before they realize they get back what they put out—and they will get back plenty if they put out plenty, or they will get back little if they put out little....(3D)

February 11

One of the greatest feelings is to accomplish a task or goal that you set out to do when others doubted your success. We are all born with the same amount of potential. It's totally up to us to determine what we do with it. A tool is nothing but a wasted opportunity if you don't put it to use. Make the most of the world around you and master your tools so you can build a brighter future...(3D)

February 12

Competition is the reason we as people have made it to the heights we have. Competition is the reason we have leaders that we follow. It is how we measure success. The only way to judge our place in life is to compare it to others who are on the same path. Competition is not always to finish in first place but to just finish. It gives us that push from behind when everything in front is against us. Having others to compete with gives us reasons to be in the race. There is no greater joy than the joy of victory over all adversity...(3D)

February 13

Don't look at love as the reason you hurt. Look at love as the reason that hurting is worth it. It is said that you don't know you love someone until that person is gone because the level of loss and or hurt that you feel is equal to the level of love you felt toward that person. However, it does not always take loss to realize what you have. Pay more attention to the ones around you and constantly show your level of appreciation. You know how much someone truly loves you by how much they show appreciation for you on a consistent basis and not just when they are down on in a time of need....(3D)

February 14

When it's hard to find a reason to keep pushing forward, look in the mirror and see all the miracles of life and your gift to the world. It is never a choice of being here or not because we already are. The choices we have are how we live through the time we have. Making decisions are the greatest gift life could bring. It is common for people to go through their entire lives questioning why they should live and never really realizing how they should live. If we were never meant to reach for the stars then we would not have been given the gift of sight to see them...(3D)

February 15

Change is the lifeblood of a happy and fruitful life. People often say "I've been doing this way forever" and then wonder why they are in the same position they started in. Loyalty certainly has its place for accolades but it is never intended to compromise change. Change is the thing that makes life interesting. It is how we grow and develop. The reason marriage is such a sacrifice is because we commit to a constant in our lives till the day of death. Life and death are the most extreme changes and everyday in-between is an opportunity for change...(3D)

February 16

To continue to stay in a relationship or situation you know is not right is bad for both people involved. It's one thing to stay in it because you feel as if you can't do it alone and a total different situation when you're doing something at your own expense to make another person happy. We all have the power to leave but few have the courage to take the first step. Do something because you feel it's right not because your told it's right...(3D)

February 17

Pain is a temporary substitution for satisfaction. We have pain so we can appreciate the good times even more. It is to be used to remind us of the hard journey we have to go through to get the objectives we want in life. When you experience pain and make it through, you become better prepared for future events. Preparation is one of the key ingredients of a prosperous life and can prevent unnecessary pain from affecting your life....(3D)

February 18

To truly be healthy you must not only work out the muscles but your brain and spirit as well. There is no point in being in the best physical shape and not knowing what is important in life. The things that are important are the things that we can't see. The most important things are feelings that are direct results of our actions. The way we make people feel when we walk in a room is more important than all the money in the world. You can't buy feelings; you can only temporarily numb them. Focus on the way you are perceived by others and you will change the way you perceive yourself....(3D)

February 19

When we always look for something or someone better than what we have we don't spend any time appreciating what we have. Because the world to most is large and gives the illusion of having more, we tend to always seek more. We should be taking a step back and evaluating everything in front of our eyes. That's not to say not to strive for better, it's simply saying that as you strive for better, take the time to look around as you travel and breathe deeply....(3D)

February 20

Love is finding the ability to forgive those who have done you wrong. It's not hard to hold a grudge. What's hard is understanding why someone wronged you. Love is a verb not a noun. It requires you to do something much more than saying, "I love you." Your love will be taken more seriously when you show it, rather than just profess it; one way of showing that love is forgiving. ...(3D)

February 21

If you find something better to do with your time, then you're probably not where you want to be in life. People that are the most successful in life are the ones who always make the best of their time. They are the ones who don't look at 9 to 5 as a chore but as an opportunity. Nothing in life is given without sacrifice. You must give to receive just like you must practice to play. Perception is the key in changing where you are and where you want to be...(3D)

February 22

It is true that it is always better to be early than late expect in the beginning and end of life. If we are born too early, we may face difficulties with health. And no one wants to be early to their own death. We are only promised that there will be an end to all of life and we only have the time we have been given right now. Punctuality is a great thing because it shows you are dependable. But putting a rush on things shows impatience and is the main reason most fail. Patience is one of the main traits of a successful predator and you must decide if you want to be the prey or the predator…(3D)

February 23

Some people desire things in life so that they won't have limitations, but even if we had wings to fly the sky is the highest we could go. Our limitations are not caused by what we have or don't have. They are the result of what we are able to imagine. Our minds can go higher than the furthest star and fit in places that have no entrances. The human is placed above all other creatures because he not only imagines but has the ability to act on what he sees in his mind. He can turn imagination into reality…(3D)

February 24

Just as we place one foot in front of another to get to the finish line, we should place one goal in front of another to achieve our dreams. We are all creatures of habit, bound by what we are able to learn and put into practice. If we change our habits then we change our results. We will never achieve new results by taking the same steps we have taken over and over again. If you want a higher paycheck, do more work. If you want to run faster, run more often. We often want more for doing the same things we have always done and fail to realize that our results are solely based on our actions...(3D)

February 25

There is no one in the world that can place limitations on your happiness. No one can tell you what will bring pleasure to your heart. Follow your heart when there is no light to see by. Others will tell you to do what made them happy, believing that it will make you happy too. But if you listen to everyone's opinion then you will soon discover that you are not living a life for yourself. If you spend time walking in other's shadows, you will never know what it's like to have sunlight warm your skin. Without sunlight there is no growth and you will be forced to stay within the confines of darkness. When you find yourself in the shadows, step to the side and look at life in a different light. When you have followed someone else's lead for a long time, but don't feel happy, step out of their path. You'll be surprised at what you find...(3D)

February 26

As long as you have a dream you have everything. Dreams fill the voids in life created by the things you want and do not have. Dreams are the things that keep the heart beating when all the odds are against you. When you dream, you make the impossible possible. In your mind, you see something happen—every detail of it. You are able to work out solutions to problems that seem like they have no answer. Dreams give you the opportunity to focus on one goal without being disturbed by all the things in the world around us. They help us block out distractions. Dream often to achieve more….(3D)

February 27

One's limitations lie with their ability to dream and to follow it. No one can prevent another from desiring things in life. No one can control what you dream. They can only alter your perception of what the results will be when you acquire your dreams. Some say that it does not matter whether or not you enjoy having reached your goal, but only if you have reached it. For some, that is true. The feeling of having accomplished something is enough. You are the only one who knows what you wanted from that dream. Perhaps, once you reach it you want to do something more with it…Don't let anyone tell you shouldn't….(3D)

February 28

Positive attitudes bring positive results. People are attracted to positive people because positivity is contagious and people want to catch it. When negative things happen in your life, they are negative because you made them so. If you can't find the positive outcome in a bad event then you are not making use of your positivity. It can transform things. If the sun never came out again, then we would have to find a way to make tomorrow a brighter day. Let the light inside of you lead the way through the darkness of a unforgiving life—a life that sometimes makes it very difficult to see the positive side of things…(3D)

February 29 (In a Leap Year)

Finding the right person to be with is a task that is often spotted with deception. We all want a mate to share the good times with and to find support in during the bad. In a rush to find this, people often choose the wrong partner. If two people are not equally enthusiastic about being with one another, then it is not a good fit. If you settle and allow the other person to dictate what your relationship will be—how affectionate it will be, how involved with one another you will be, how communicative you will be—you will forever be yearning for more. Seek a partner with an open mind and never settle for a partially filled heart….(3D)

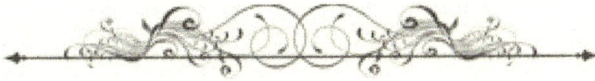

Questions

1. Describe the feelings and emotions you want to experience every day.

2. What would you like to see more of in your current/future relationship that you are not seeing today?

3. How do you plan on growing spiritually?

March

March 1

When you allow yourself to see the dark, it becomes darker. Light comes from darkness just like success comes from failure, because someone saw the light in the darkness and fostered it, and someone saw the potential for success in a failure and fostered that. Stand tall when others lay down in defeat and you will be able to see further and make better decisions. If you fear what you can't see or can't understand, then you can never truly discover what you are capable of accomplishing. If you face your fears, they will soon be behind you forever. They won't be fears anymore because you took the time to explore them and understand them and once they are not foreign to you, they are not fears. You can always learn from what's placed behind you to get through what will be in front of you…(3D)

March 2

There is nothing more important for the soul than relationships. We all are guilty of overlooking this importance until the relationship is over or has taken a turn for the worse. The people that are around us become even more important in the beginning and end of our lives. In the beginning, we need them to help mold our lives and in the end we need them for comfort. Always take advantage of opportunities to enhance your relationships and use a magnifying glass to discover their true significance in your life…..(3D)

March 3

Do things in life that you can expect favorable results from. If you ever start something with no set plan as to when you will finish it, then you set yourself up for failure because you will constantly tell yourself, "Well, I can keep putting this off. There is no due date." There will only be great outcomes when you cannot *wait* to accomplish the goal. You determine the outcome of your efforts by judging your level of expectation. You still may fall short of your desired results if your anticipation is not followed by precise steps working toward your objectives. You first have to desire, then satisfy that desire by working towards it…(3D)

March 4

Time is said to heal all wounds. Wounds are the direct result of someone taking advantage of a weakness. Our hearts become wounded when we allow love to take control of our actions and reactions. When love is in control, we no longer have the power to make conscious decisions and we are incapable of seeing that what we are doing will harm us. We act on pure emotion and most of the time, this only ends in pain. Time has the ability to heal all wounds, but it can also make wounds worse if they are not tended to correctly. Don't let time dictate how much you will hurt. Meet the cause of the wounds halfway and deal with it—do what you can to lessen the pain—so its effects will be short lived….(3D)

March 5

The things that are the most important to you are going to cause the most pain when lost. But there is a purpose behind experiencing deep pain—it prepares us for the small losses and inconveniences of everyday life. Pain is an opportunity to grow and sorrow is an opportunity to reflect. If we never forget then we never truly lose—that is why it is said that people who have passed live on in our memories. We can turn a loss into an opportunity if we understand how to transform energy into different forms. Turn grievance into love by redirecting that energy towards loving the things you have and rather than grieving the things you have lost…(3D)

March 6

Look for new ways to express your love. You can show someone how much you love them in different ways. You can take time to learn different things that put a smile on their face. If you are a person who never holds hands, grab your loved one's hand while walking. Come home and give your loved one a kiss. Do something that you just don't normally do because, while love is natural, its expression is rare….(3D)

March 7

Too much of anything sweet soon turns sour. That's why we must never over indulge in things we love. Taking more than we need will only lead to displeasure of what we once loved. Too much love is not good because we can end up loving something or someone more than ourselves. This can cause great harm not only to ourselves but also to the ones we love because they have to watch our downfall that is a direct result of us loving them. The giant loved the mouse so much he accidentally squeezed it to death. The mouse was literally suffocated by the giant's love...(3D)

March 8

If you live with great intentions, then your efforts will always be justified. Sometimes we do things that hurt others, when our intentions were to benefit them. We are judged more on our intent than our actual actions because our intent is based on what we feel in our hearts. Always follow your heart and your regrets will be far and few in between because even if things go wrong, you know that your intentions were always pure...(3D)

March 9

We always want time to pass when things are bad and wish we could extend it when things are great. But we should be grateful for time, whether it is good or bad because it is something that we can never get back. Time is precious and can never be bought or sold for any amount of money. Don't spend this valuable resource foolishly, wishing it would go by faster. Find ways to take advantage of it and complete the tasks now that you had planned to do later, because there may not be a later...(3D)

March 10

Scars are roadmaps of life and all its twist and turns. Scars are the result of how you have healed from wounds. They are a constant reminder of what paths should remain untraveled. When we look at another's scars we can also see the strength of the individual. Those scars tell a complete story of what the person went through. More importantly, they tell how the person has recovered. It can be beneficial to have scars from the past, but don't let the past scar your future...(3D)

March 11

Persistence is the backbone of success. It is the core of all things gained in life. The more you consistently pursue your goals, the closer they become. Success is measured by how persistent you are and how resilient you are against defeat. You can't always determine your future but you can determine how much effort you are willing to put into your plan...(3D)

March 12

Just because you're alive, that does not mean you are living. Live life with a desire to experience things and an understanding of death and your life will be filled with an abundance of joy. We are meant to work to live not live to work. Our destination is determined by the bridges we build and mountains we climb. And our failure is determined by the valleys we walk and rivers we swim. The ability to transcend is learned through lessons taught in the school of life. The more you pay attention, the better your grade will be and even greater the reward for your success...(3D)

March 13

In life we strive to surround ourselves with people and things that bring comfort. Whether they be relationships, money, cars, or clothes, we search for things that will bring us comfort and make life easier. Working hard for the things you want allows you to keep them. If they are ever lost, you know how to regain them. A rich man is forever rich if he never forgets how he gained his wealth….(3D)

March 14

To know your own flaws and weaknesses is to know your own strengths and perfections. Everyone is born with imperfections that they are meant to work on. We are driven to correct our flaws and while making these corrections our eyes open up to the flaws of others and we learn to accept more people. To build a perfect person would be impossible because we all have our views of perfection based on our own imperfections. The reason lady justice has a blindfold on is because you can't judge a person fairly if you use your eyes. You must start with the heart and the mind will follow….(3D)

March 15

Things tend to get worse when you expect them to. Expecting the worst situation brings the worst situation. That's not to say if you plan for the best that the best will happen, but you can be assured that hoping for the worst will never yield the best. We bring onto ourselves what we put out. If you want good things to happen in your life, expect them to. Don't allow negative thoughts to take up any room in your mind. Save that space for positive energy that produces positive results…(3D)

March 16

Be prepared for success all of the time because the day and time of your last breath cannot be known. If you are always prepared for success—if you seek for opportunities for it everywhere you look—then you never allow time to be a hindrance but instead, an ally.

Time can be your greatest companion if you are always ready to accept and deal with all the things that come with it. To prepare is to be aware and if you act on things that you are aware of, this is called being proactive. Don't sit back and allow things to come to you. Seek them out and meet them halfway so you always have the advantage…(3D)

March 17

People often say hurtful words to others because they are displacing hurt that is within them. Some of us are strong enough to endure words that are cast upon us by others. But some are affected deeply by strong words. The longer you allow hurtful words to affect you, the deeper the hole becomes and the harder it becomes to climb out of it. Listen to the words others say to hurt you but be a rubber band, not a sponge. Let them bounce off after you take them in. That way they won't affect you in the long run, unlike a sponge who takes in and holds onto everything until it has to release...The equivalent of that release in a person is a breakdown….(3D)

March 18

The greatest difficulty of man is the ability to put someone before your self. We are born with instincts that tell us to look out for ourselves above others—these are our survival instincts. This means that we are born to strive for the number one position but most people allow other people to put blinders on this fact. Because we are designed to strive to be number one, we have a hard time putting others first. It takes a great deal of sacrifice to allow this to take place. Sacrifice is one of the main things that separate us from animals. To sacrifice by putting another before yourself is a great struggle that comes with great reward…(3D)

March 19

Gifts make people smile for a day and experiences make people laugh forever, whenever they are down. Give things to others to remind them how much you care. Experience things with others that you want to remember. Life is full of experiences that you can learn from and others that can help you grow. Take from your experiences the gifts—the knowledge—that you want to give others. Share with them but remember that it's not up to you what they take from it. It's only your choice to share the experience and give others the opportunity to learn from it….(3D)

March 20

Nothing matters more than doing your best at all you do. No one will ever fault you for doing the most that you can. Overachieving is doing more than others expect from you. That's what makes society grow as a whole. When you work harder than others expected you to then you receive more from your work than others expected. Society is based on what is contributed to it by the individuals that make it up. If you just give what is expected, then society will return the favor. You will always remain just average or below…(3D)

March 21

To live is to experience and to experience you have to live. The one thing that sets us apart from others is our experiences—the things we go through to get where we want to be. Staring fear in the face and taking risks is the only way to gain confidence. Fear can help save our lives or it can limit us by changing the way we think—by making us think that *less* is possible. And when we think less is possible, we try less…(3D)

March 22

There is nothing more precious than the time we have right now. Time is never on our side but it is always at our disposal. It is up to us to decide how to best use it or it will get the best of us. We will wake up one day and realize we don't have what we want, and we don't have the time any more to achieve it. We try to put life into perspective and focus on the important things, but we often allow the less important things to take up our time. When we lose track of what our purpose is then we lose sight of what will bring true joy to our hearts. We find joy by achieving goals that we set in pursuit of our dreams…(3D)

March 23

It all comes down to who you are able to touch while you are here. You can't take anything physical with you when you die, you can only have *left* something, whether that be an impression, memories, or possessions for those who come after you. It's a hard pill to swallow. Don't allow anyone to tell you how to live your life. Time is limited and you will end up realizing you want to live life your way. So trying to live it based on someone else's advice will only be a waste of time. It's to take advice that keeps you on your path, but don't take advice that will steer you away from your goals….(3D)

March 24

When there is no room to travel further down in your life, then you know that you are very close to achievement. It's easiest to realize what you have in life when you are at a low point. When things are going well people will pretend to be kind to you, when they only want something in return. It is only in moments of solitude when you can analyze who has good intentions for you. If you set small goals you know you can accomplish then the large ones will never be too difficult. That's why they are called steps not leaps...(3D)

March 25

The ones who become great sources of inspiration and motivation are the ones who tell their story of triumph. You must walk through the fire and come out the other side with all your worries burned off your flesh. Those that don't push to get out of the fire have their flesh melted and are left to burn. We all try to avoid the fire altogether but from the ashes grows life. To progress and build anew it is necessary to shed the old. But there is a limit to how much you should shed. Never allow yourself to get caught up in removing too much of yourself. Be conscious of what is weighing you down—what is excess—and what traits are actually necessary to achieve your goal. If you become obsessed with changing and shedding, when you look in the mirror you might not recognize who you are improving upon...(3D)

March 26

Taking chances means realizing an opportunity when it presents itself. A chance is a calculated risk. When you take a chance you understand all the possible outcomes of your decision and you are willing to deal with the consequences, whether good or bad. We take chances everyday by walking outside, so why not take a chance in following your dreams? The worst thing that could happen is to find out that your dream is not really what it's cracked up to be. But the sooner you learn what it is exactly that you are asking for, then the sooner you can realize your actual goal. Find people that are in the position you want to be in and ask them what it's like and what it takes. Only then will you know if the chance is worth your time, and if the possible positive outcome is worth the risk of the negative outcome....(3D)

March 27

If you allow your faith to guide you through the difficult times, then joy will be the result on the other side. If you keep faith no matter how hard it gets, then you will never lose sight of your goal. Faith will allow you to do things that others think is impossible. Faith will knock down the walls of ignorance and doubt. If you want to be a champion, master your faith and resist disbelief. You will keep your head held high when it feels as if the weight of the world is pulling you down....(3D)

March 28

When you decide to make a major change in your life for the better, do it with authority and certitude. The more certain you are about making a defining change, the greater impact that change will have on your life. Looking back can only be useful if you can understand the mistakes you have made, so that you may avoid them. Keep your eyes on what you want to become and allow the things in your past to be stepping stools to get there…(3D)

March 29

Take time out in your life to fight for what you want and what you think you deserve…No one ever gives people their dreams on a silver platter. Normally, things that are *not* furthering our goals take up most of our time, e.g. people who drag us down, a job that we don't want. You have to work hard, carve out time, and work late at night if you you're going to find the time to get what you want. You must learn how to defend yourself and your dreams. They are yours and no one should take them from you. You must learn to fight temptation and fight against all the people that will try and get you off course. You must resist the desire to keep falterers in your life who tell you, "You've done the most you can do." You must learn to fight for your position and fight to achieve the results you want. The best way to learn how to fight is to learn how to defend. If you have great defense no one will ever be able to beat you if you are willing to fight for what you want….(3D)

March 30

Success is measured by how many people you are able to bless with what you have achieved. This could mean you are successful because you have accumulated enough money to help those in need, or it could mean you have accumulated knowledge that you can share with others. But you can always tell how successful you are by how many people you are able to reach through your new success. It's all a matter of how much you are willing to give, not how much you are able to attain....(3D)

March 31

It is said that you should never believe what you hear and you should only believe half of what you see. So, you should focus on developing your listening skills twice as much as you do your visual skills. What you see is already one step ahead of what you hear because what you're looking at is processed. All you have to do is determine what you are looking at. You must rely on your memory to tell you what it exactly is. When you hear something, not only must you determine what the combination of words means but you must also decipher tone of voice, voice inflections and the accent. From there, you determine what was intended and how it was intended to be said. You also must determine how much of it is the truth and how you are going to respond. So, believe half of what you see because it's too late not to look, and believe none of what you hear because you control what you are listening too. Sometimes silence speaks louder than noise....(3D)

Questions

1. What reputation do you want to have with family and friends?

2. How often would you like to exercise each week? And for how long?

3. How do you want to be remembered by your family? Peers? And people who have never met you?

April

April 1

There is no higher motivation than love. People will do things they thought impossible when they do them for love. Love can make you feel like a cloud in the sky or a rock under the ground. But it does something nothing else can. It can make you feel that you would be willing to give up everything for its sake. True love is always defined by what you are willing to sacrifice for it. The more you are willing to sacrifice, the more you love. Love is natural and undefined by any bounds. Let love find its place in your heart and your love will spread its effects to others who lack it…(3D)

April 2

Nobody takes a shot in basketball expecting it not to go in. So why do people take chances in life if they don't expect them to work out for the best? There is no point in doing something if you don't expect it to benefit you. It's like practicing and thinking that the practice won't help you out during the game…it does not make sense to perform half way and expect the most from life. Give it your all and expect to get it all. You are what you think you are. If you want to be the best you must believe you are even before you see the results…(3D)

April 3

Never take for granted the things you have today because the things you have today can easily be the things you miss tomorrow. If you tell yourself there will always be more time to do something, you'll have unfulfilling days and nights full of unattained dreams. You have been given the chance to do it right now. If you wait, then you are playing a dangerous game of time roulette and hoping that fate does not take its course before you are ready to take action. The only way to prepare for the future is to act on it right now....(3D)

April 4

If you ask for something you really want, it will come. Have faith without discernment. That means faith that doesn't waver because things look good or bad one day. Ask and believe you will receive something and you will. You only have to ask for it once, but believe every moment that it will come. If you ask for something more than once, that is a sign that your faith has wavered. If you ask for something and spend your time planning what you'll do when it comes, then you will be prepared to receive it. If you don't prepare for something that you have asked for, it may be taken away or pass you by just as fast as it came to you.....(3D)

April 5

It is a difficult line to walk when you desire to be the best, but are afraid to be better than others. But there is no point in doing anything if you do not strive to do your best. No one can push you to want to be the best but yourself. It has to come from within. But in the process to become the best you must not think that you are better than the next person. Ego can either take you to new heights or break you down to nothing. Knowing that you deserve just as much respect at the next person, and no more, will keep your ego and pride in check......(3D)

April 6

Loving someone requires that you also accept their flaws. For you to love a sport you play you must also enjoy the practice, the training and all the conditioning it takes to be in shape just to play the game. To love a person, you must accept all the things you don't like about them and be willing to find a way to overlook them, rather than try to change them. If you try to change the requirements to play the game—if you try to find ways to skip over the practice—or the things you don't like about someone you are not truly loving the game or person. You are in love with the thought of it or them. But love is understanding, accepting and forgiving. First decide if you want to love before you decide who or what you love.....(3D)

April 7

The Colorado River was able to carve out the magnificent Grand Canyon because it mastered the art of staying low. To become great in life you must learn how to be the lowest in the crowd and have the loudest voice without speaking a word. It doesn't necessarily take a loud voice to be heard. Be the one whose actions are seen and accomplishments recognized....(3D)

April 8

The most successful people are the ones who know when they do not know something—ones who know their limitations. Pretending you know something is the quickest way to failure. People who pretend to know things and act as they do attract people who pretend to be friends. But when something happens and you need a friend to lend a hand, then you will find out that your friends were only *pretending* that they knew how to be there for you....(3D)

April 9

To live is to be soft and supple. To die is to become hard and brittle. The hardest weapon will be broken the easiest and the hardest of wood is easiest to knock down in the slightest of wind. So if you strive to be the hardest and most mighty then you fail in your pursuit of success. But if you open your mind and heart and speak with lively words then your actions will remain fluid and move in the direction of success...(3D)

April 10

It is much wiser to act, achieve success but to not take the credit. When you act to gain acknowledgment and not because it is the right thing to do, the only thing you gain is self-destruction through self-indulgence. If you fill yourself with credit, then if things fall apart, you will not be prepared to pay the consequences. If you do things because you want to, then accomplishments will never yield an interest rate you cannot afford to pay....(3D)

April 11

To succeed in life you must focus on your obligations and tend to them because they are the most important things in your life. Obligations are your motivation to push forward. People who do not attend to their own obligations end up spending their time attending to other's mistakes. This makes all the true and straight things they say seem crooked. To become successful you must learn to follow through with your obligations and allow those who criticize and magnify others mistakes to take the back seat to real virtue…(3D)

April 12

Life is all about challenges and triumphs. A loss is only considered a loss if you fail to gain something from it. Positivity sprouts from every negative seed if it is watered with desire and left to sit in the light of determination. You can determine how and what you take from situations, but one thing you can never get back is the time spent going through it. So make sure it's worth it because wasted time is wasted opportunity and wasted opportunity is the quickest path to failure…(3D)

April 13

Will power is the ability to withstand all odds in order to get the results you want. It is allowing nothing to keep you from your dreams. Will power is the result of inner strength. It is the strength that stays when everything seems to fall apart. It is the reason you push forward when all others say there is no way. Will power is faith working in all the ways it is intended to work. Without will power there would be no advancement, because there is always a reason to quit. Find your will power and use it to make a way….(3D)

April 14

It is said that, with faith any dreams can be accomplished. A person's limitations are set by their own will to live the life they dream of. They are not what others dream is possible for you but what you are able to dream. We all want things in our lives but few take action to get them. To know one's limitations is to know the limits of the world around us. We all can imagine but few ever learn how to make imagination into reality. However, we are all given the same tools to make it such…(3D)

April 15

To gain you must give. To win you must work. To succeed you must fail. There is no reward for wanting other than depression and worry. Results and rewards of substance are given to those of us who put forth the effort to achieve them. We are products and the direct result of what our parents and society had to go through. The miracles of life are the effects of transformed energy. We come from a greater source of energy and are direct descendants of great people who came before us. We wouldn't be here if they had not succeeded. If they did not make it through their struggles we would not have the luxuries that we all enjoy every day…(3D)

Sometimes you'll be given the chance for immediate, but short-lived, gratification. If you are able to pass on that to continue working towards your greater goal, you have proven the strength of your willpower. But you also have to learn how to recognize when your actual goal is in front of you. If you are looking for a particular type of job and it is offered to you, but at a lower salary than you had expected, you have to know what is more important to you, i.e. the nature of the work, or the amount of money. You also have to know when it is realistic to keep waiting. So, you get the job you want, but it isn't exactly what you thought it would be like. But you can't always choose what form you will receive your goal in. The only choice you have is to accept the gift when it arrives...(3D)

April 16

You shouldn't jump on every opportunity that seems like it will lead you to your goal. The means to the end do matter, and if you take an opportunity that compromises your ethics then you will not be as happy when you achieve your goal. You should also avoid taking opportunities that you feel forced to decide on quickly. When our backs are up against a wall, it is not the best time to make a decision that will have long-term effects on us. When we are at a low point and things really aren't going our way, this is when we will feel particularly tempted to make a rash decision and jump on an opportunity. But it's that time—when our minds are weak—that we have to be strong at heart....(3D)

April 17

You learn what's best by trying different things. You cannot identify the correct method until you've tried the wrong ones. Be wary of the paths you take in an attempt to reach your end goal. If you go too fast, you might be thrown off when you reach a sharp turn. If you go too slowly, then you might miss out on opportunity. Move with a persistent but cautious step so that when you fall, you can at least know that you did everything you could and that the fall was you're your fault...(3D)

April 18

Challenges are just opportunities to become better. When you are faced with them you can either fight through them and turn them into victories, or run away from them and turn them into defeats. People that you look up to are usually the ones who fought through most challenges. People who tell you something cannot be done are usually those who ran away from challenges and never even tried. Don't listen to them, because they never even made the attempt to fight through a challenge, so they know nothing about what it takes. You must fight to become better. Running from challenges only leaves you in the exact same place...(3D)

April 19

Most of the time things get much worse before they get better. That is life's way of testing your will and faith. If you weather the storm there is always a rainbow waiting for you when it's over. But what is at the end of the rainbow is determined by the caliber of work that you put in to trying to reach it. Think about a pot of coal. Its value can be increased by adding great pressure and heat until it turns into a diamond. Or it can be used to fuel a fire. Its value depends on the work you put into it...(3D)

April 20

Anything we have that is of value started as a thought, and desire turned it into a dream. That dream was realized when effort was backed by an unwavering determination, meaning, you let nothing prevent or deter you from your dream. If you had it would have just remained a dream. You determine what you want it to be. People thought it would be impossible to talk to someone who was miles away until Edison dreamt up a telephone. They also thought flying was a crazy idea until the Wright brothers dreamt up the airplane. Sometimes people call your dreams crazy. But those are the people who don't believe in their own dreams and just take life as it is, rather than making life what they want it to be...(3D)

April 21

If you base your work on an expected amount of payment then your expectations will always be greater than your results. You must always work with intensions to do the best job and your reward will come in multiple forms including money from unexpected sources. Reward is always given to those who put in work and follow through until they get the desired results. Find ways to excel when it seems you have hit the limit. We all have opportunity to do great things if we put in great effort matched with determination...(3D)

April 22

Anger is a result of letting something bother you to the point that you can't control your actions. This is when your thoughts are expressed in outward aggression and turn into unintended, hurtful actions towards people and things you did not really intend to hurt. When you feel as if you are at that point of anger you should separate yourself from others and find a place within yourself to calm down. Think about what you really want to say before expressing your thoughts. By doing this, you will save your relationships and your intensions will not be misunderstood....(3D)

April 23

As you begin to turn a new page in life never forget the words on the page before because when you get to the next one you may be lost. Get into the story and become the main character. Only then will you understand what the author was trying to depict. Every book has a meaning and purpose that is trapped between the first and last chapter. Turn each page in the book of life with a desire to find its true purpose. Don't be in a great rush to get to the last page. Enjoy all the hard work that was put in between, and recognize the connections between one page and the next, and the progression. Your main goal in life should be to find definition to unclear objectives—to find a pattern and a process to achieve your goals....(3D)

April 24

Excuses are the building blocks of an unsuccessful life. The more you use them, the higher the wall becomes that prevents you from reaching your goals. Excuses are used when we are not willing to do all that it takes to get to where we want to be. We use them to explain why we are in the situation we are currently in and why we can't get out of it. Or rather, to make it seem like we can't get out of it. Once we get into the habit of using excuses they just keep coming and become a way of life. If you think about what you say before you open your mouth and let an excuse out, you might be able to stop the wall from being built. Sometimes it's better to not say nothing at all then to allow excuses to represent who you are...(3D)

April 25

When you get some bad news that you really don't want to hear, let it affect you for 5 minutes then let it go. I know it's easier said than done but once you are able to, all bad things you come across will not affect you for long. They say good always comes with some bad, and you can choose how much of the bad you want to affect your days. Only think about it for as long as it takes for you to let the news digest, but then think of some way to overcome it or make the best of it. Use things in your life that bring joy to counter things in your life that bring pain....(3D)

April 26

People judge how others are doing by looking at their outside appearance and how they carry themselves. We tend to lean on these people when we have an issue or problem. But being a crunch is draining. Don't let others weigh you down with their problems unless they are people who are willing to help you in return with your problems. If they only take from you, you will not have enough strength to handle your own issues. Sometimes you must tell people you can't listen to their problems because once you do, they become your problems. People want you to share in their problems because a problem divided is much easier to overcome. That is understandable but choose which battles you take on with others. Help the friends who provide support you in return, or else you will lose your strength....(3D)

April 27

Sometimes it's best to just push the "rest" button on our lives. It's easy to keep doing what you know is wrong just because you are getting away with it and because you don't know what other path to take. This is when it's time to push the "rest" button. If you stay on the wrong path it is only a matter of time before it all comes to an end. There is no such thing as an old bad boy or girl because they don't last that long. The longer you do things that are wrong, the sooner you will fall from your phony success. To succeed or gain in negativity is to lose or fail morally…(3D)

April 28

Respect is something you earn by giving it out. In order for someone else to understand you and respect you then you must learn that people respect where respect is due. You always know if you have been disrespected because there is a sense of deep hurt to your pride. Pride lets you know when you are disrespected and it will also let you know who you should respect. Age does not guarantee you respect. It's those that learn to respect others over time that ends up deserving to be respected when they are older. It makes sense if you think about it. A person has to know a thing or two (like who to respect) to even survive to a certain age. *That* is why we respect our elderly. They knew what to do to grow old…(3D)

April 29

When someone does something to you that makes you upset try to find something nice you can do for them. When someone has hurt you and they know they have hurt you, they expect you to retaliate. If you do the opposite and do something nice, they well be left feeling even worse for what they did. Kill anger with kindness and your heart will be filled with more joy then vengeance….(3D)

April 30

Motivation comes from stimulation. Put yourself in places with people and events that will inspire you and provide models of what you hope to attend. It's great to be motivated by your dreams, but if you can put yourself in real life situations that will motivate you, even better….(3D)

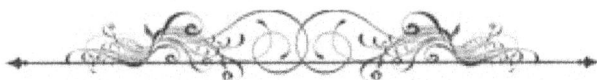

Questions

1. What impact do you want to have on your community?

2. What groups or organizations would you like to join?

3. What special skill or trade would you like to learn how to do?

May

May 1

If you don't know what and who true friends are, then look and see who is around you when you're at the lowest point in your life. If you want to know who and what will bring you down when you're at the top, keep in mind the people who are only around when things are going well for you. The saying "more money, more problems" exists because the higher you get in life, the more people will show up who want to take things from you. No one likes to feel inferior to anyone else, so they bring you down to where they are, sometimes even lower. Be aware of who you tell when things are going well, because they could easily be the reason things soon go bad...(3D)

May 2

Some people will never feel success because they do not know how to measure success. Success is not being the richest person in the world. Success is finding what it is that makes you happy and pursuing it until it is finally reached. Success is the result of hard work and effort. You can't be successful if you cannot pull yourself up after failure. Success requires knowing what you want and never giving up until you reach it. It comes when you reach your goals, and that comes when you can get up after falling...(3D)

May 3

If you know your limitations, then you will never be caught off guard by your failures. Also, if you know your limits, then you will not allow others to take advantage of you. People take advantage of those who don't know their limits; those who do not know how much they can safely do, or give, and so they keep doing or giving until they break. It's like knowing how much weight a bridge can hold. You would never put more weight on it than it could handle, but if you don't know the weight limit the bridge will fall unexpectedly....(3D)

May 4

Always seek perfection because if you fall short you will still be better than most. You will get more than most if you push for what others can only dream about. If you spend your time making your dreams come true then you won't ever have time to think about not making them come true, and it is those thoughts that hold you back. The only thing that can stop you from reaching your goals is you and your negative thoughts. Don't allow the person in the mirror to be your hindrance. Instead, make that person your inspiration....(3D)

May 5

You know when you love someone when you admire their flaws. When the things that make them unique are the things that make you smile. Love is something that is organic and grows with time, so the longer you are with someone, your love will either grow or it will wither away. When you love someone, they have the ability to hurt you. That is love's greatest flaw. When you love someone, they can lift you when you are down and calm you when you're upset. Take the time to learn what love is and you will learn how to take care of it so it never leaves…(3D)

May 6

Work is like pushing a boulder up a hill; it is hard to get going, and the closer you get to the top, the harder it is to push. Success is when you get to the top after that last push and the boulder begins to roll down the other side by itself. If you put in the work to make it to the top, not much more work will be required once you get there. But it is easy for you to start rolling back down the side that you climbed up with the slightest push. So once you get to your goal set another one and start pushing again. That way you never have to worry about rolling back down because you already started climbing upward again….(3D)

May 7

A great tragedy always brings people together. This is because we feel comfort when we know others are going through the same thing we are. Dividing a problem makes it easier to overcome than trying to handle it alone. The same should hold true in times of great triumph. There is no point in success if it is not divided among people who have not reached that point. You cannot really feel success until you share it with others….(3D)

May 8

Use the things in life that momentarily brought you down as stepping stools to move forward. When you can't find a way to get to where you want to go, remember your past downfalls and realize that they actually helped get you to places of triumph. The only reason you will fail is that you give up. Giving up is the fastest way to get to the bottom. Giving up is the main trait of a failure. Saying you are "trying" is the first step to giving up. Never say you are trying. Say you are *doing,* because saying you are trying is the same as saying you are giving up soon…(3D)

May 9

Being faithful to someone in a relationship means exactly what it sounds like, being full of faith. You must have total belief that you do not have to go elsewhere for satisfaction, because your partner will continue loving you and satisfying you. Your partner in turn will continue to remain faithful—full of faith that you will continue loving and satisfying them—and they will not go elsewhere. Surround yourself with people whose actions fill you with faith, and you will remain faithful to them….(3D)

May 10

Most people don't succeed because they don't want to pay the price for success. What is that price? It's saying no to instant gratification and quick fixes. It's passing up on small, immediate pleasures so you have time to work towards a larger, more sustainable pleasure. It is a price that is constantly rising if you are standing still—if you are not doing something every day to work towards your success. It is much better to pay for it now than to wait and wake up one day to realize, *I'm not where I thought I would be at this point in my life. And I have SO much work to do to get there.* There is never a sale price on success because, like with anything, value goes down with price. But you can guarantee that if you do pay the full price you will get exactly what you pay for ....success in realizing your dreams...(3D)

May 11

If you search for a way long and hard enough you will find it. Things have a way of presenting themselves when you are looking for them, but that doesn't always mean you'll be happy when they do. Like in a relationship, for example, when you are looking for a sign that your partner is being unfaithful, you will find it. You will find it because you look for it in everything your partner does and says. You will find it because you can *interpret* things anyway you like. In times of job loss, if you constantly look for work you will find it. You will find it because you'll take *any* job, so you tell yourself that *any* job that comes along is the one you want. What we want and ask for eventually comes, because we tell ourselves it has arrived. We tell ourselves *this job makes me happy* when perhaps it doesn't. We tell ourselves *my partner is cheating* when perhaps he isn't. We can talk, dream or interpret anything into our lives, when we are too afraid to wait for the real thing. There's a reason we're told to be careful with what we ask for...(3D)

May 12

The day you stop learning should be the day you stop breathing. Use every sunrise as an opportunity to learn and every sunset as an opportunity to reflect on the lessons learned. Information comes to us in many forms but our application of information is what causes it to become knowledge. Don't just live life. Don't let a piece of information be born and die with you. Contemplate what you learn; store it away, categorize it, and see how it connects to everything else. Turn it into something more useful, find the layers in it. That is your job—to make today's information *more* useful to those that will come after you. Just as those who came before you made their findings more useful for you. This is the only chance we have at avoiding downfalls—learning form others who have been down that path before. Spend every day continuing to build on that path….(3D)

May 13

Nothing in life is more important than understanding self-worth. When you lose sight of how much you are truly worth, then you can't understand how important you are to others. You lose sight of how you could be helpful to others, and so you've lost sight of your biggest purpose in life. Each and every person makes our society what it is, whether that's good or bad at times. When one person is removed or taken away, the influence of the person is also removed. No one is born without a purpose. Whether we are here for a few minutes or 100 years, we all have a purpose. Life is all about the search for it, so that we can ensure we do *more* of it…(3D)

May 14

If you want to make changes, if you want to move forward, stop and reflect on where you have been and what you have been through. Sometimes, in order to move forward in the right direction, you should look in your rear view mirror first to make sure the cars that you have passed are still behind you—that your tribulations are still in your past. If you allow them to be in your present then you are sure to run into them again, and again they will prevent you from going in the direction you need to go in…(3D)

May 15

Never give up hope because hope is like the heart; it keeps the blood of determination flowing through your veins, and without that blood, you cannot take any sort of action. If you stop thinking that there is a way, if you lose hope, then all possible roads to victory will be closed, because *your hope* paved those roads. It always takes time for desired results to manifest. Time is something that we cannot control, and we don't *like* to be without control. When you feel out of control and as if time is passing too slowly, think of what you can control. We can control how and what we do in the time while we are waiting. When you are waiting to hear back from one job, apply to others. When you are waiting to hear if your partner has cheated on you, surround yourself with friends and family; cultivate the relationships that are steadfast in your life. The more we are actively pursuing our goals the closer they come within our reach…(3D)

May 16

Being great is a product of taking advantage of opportunity. Opportunities happen when you make the decision to allow circumstance to be helpful. The result of your decision shows how well you were able to understand the situation and handle it. Most of these situations can be handled quite well if you take the time to understand everything about them. Be patient in making your decisions and allow your heart to lead in times that the mind may be lost…(3D)

May 17

Don't worry about the negative things people say about you. Use them as catapults to reach greater heights. People will not always tell you the things you want to hear but they will tell you things that you need to hear. The negative should make the positive even more influential because the people who made negative comments will be even more surprised by the positive outcome. People who tell you negative things are often trying to displace negative feelings they are having about themselves. They are projecting their feelings onto you. It makes people feel good to downgrade others because it gives them a sense of power. But that is a power that soon dissipates. Like cells in a battery, the more you use them the faster they die….(3D)

May 18

There will come a time when your will and determination will be tested by the pride and discouragement of others. People will attempt to deter you from your dreams and the more you are determined, the more they will try to alter your course. It's not about how many hurdles you knock down. It's more about how many you remove before you get to them. The path will be designed to make you fall because character is built by the way you hold your ground when difficulty comes your way…(3D)

May 19

Not only must you start from somewhere but you must start from somewhere that will lead to somewhere greater. Put your first foot forward and follow it with the other. You can't start running until you learn to walk. You have to learn how to climb up steps before you reach the mountaintop. Allow determination to push you toward your desires. Goals are stages along the way that you must continue to conquer or you will be held there until you do. Don't let your goals become pits of regret because you set your expectations too high. Be realistic in your immediate aims and ambitious in your ultimate desires...(3D)

May 20

Family is the backbone that gives strength to life. All difficult things are eased with the slightest soft touch or word from a family member. But family does not always come in the form of relatives. Sometimes it comes to us as friends or neighbors. But family can always be found when you are in need of a shoulder to lean on or a couch to lay on. Family is the reason for all wars and the cause of all peace. We are only as strong as the family ties we have and the relationships we build. Express your love to your family and their love will bring meaning to your life everyday...(3D)

May 21

The sunshine shines at night; it just depends on where you are standing on earth. Your positioning determines whether or not you will be warmed by its rays. If you cannot see the light, then look in a different direction and stand in a different place. Darkness is just an opportunity to brighten an area that is being shaded by neglect. Sometimes we all need to bring light to areas in our life that we often shade with neglect. Don't allow problems to grow into nights of worry when you can turn them into days of sunshine…(3D)

May 22

Love is something that you must never force. It is like holding sand in your hand. If you try to grasp it too tightly, the sand begins to fall through your fingers. The harder you squeeze, the faster it falls from your grasp. Accept it when it comes to you but never assume it's there. You will know if it is right because nothing else will compare and the person you love will feel the same….(3D)

May 23

We all want to make it to the top as fast as possible but to get there we must go through trials and tribulations. Starting from the bottom and working your way up is the best way to guarantee you will remain at the top once you are there. It may seem like it is taking forever to get there but all that time is necessary to learn the lessons that life has in store for us. Action will lead to more action and the harder you work towards the goals you have set, the greater you will enjoy the fruits of your labor…(3D)

May 24

There is a fine line between having too much pride and setting standards. Let your standards be set by what you feel you need in life to be comfortable. Let your pride be set by what you need in life to keep your head held high no matter how low you may become. Finding a middle ground between the two will lead to a healthier and more productive life…(3D)

May 25

Things don't always work out how we want them to. They work out how they are supposed to. We can't control what will happen if we don't take care of what's happening right now. Don't think that if you leave things alone they will get better. They won't. Things only get better if you do something about them. They won't necessarily work out the way you want them to, but they can get better. Think about how you got into the situation and work backward to get out of it. When you trace your steps you will see where you took the wrong path and be able to alter your course in the future…(3D)

May 26

Watch the tone of your voice when you speak because your intentions may be different than what your voice portrays. Most of the time it's not what you say but how you say it that tells people your intentions. If you are apologizing for something but use a sarcastic tone then your apology will probably not be accepted. Listen to the way you talk to others and watch their reactions. You will find that most react to the method not the message…(3D)

May 27

No one has ever faulted a person for trying. When one quits, it is definitely their own fault. There is no point in starting something you never plan on finishing. The ability to see it through is called courage. Courage will carry you when there is no one to lean on. Even when the lion was looking for courage while walking down the yellow brick road he discovered that he had it all the time. It is something we are born with but needs to be developed so we are prepared for what life brings us...(3D)

May 28

The most creative and innovative ideas have come to us when times are the roughest. That is because they come out of necessity. We tend to think about new ways of doing things when the regular ways are just out of our reach. When things are easy and given to us we don't try to enhance them because we become content. Contentment causes us to be caught off guard when something bad happens. If we constantly think about what we can do to improve our situations then we will never be worried when the carpet is removed from under our feet. We will know we have methods to move forward…(3D)

May 29

Once discouragement has set into your mind then the smallest thing will block your path. You begin to come up with reasons and excuses as to why you are not able to do things and these excuses become bricks that are bonded with discouragement. The higher you build this wall, the more energy you will need to climb over it. Energy being faith that is generated from confidence. Believe that the gifts you were given can take you where you want to go and don't allow the foundation of discouragement to ever set…(3D)

May 30

When someone tells you that you can't do something, use it as motivation to do what you believe you can. If you always listen when others say something is impossible, you will never realize what you are capable of doing. Anything is possible if you believe it can be done and you work towards your goal. You never know where your efforts will lead or who they will help and inspire. Do good work to reap good rewards. There is no greater feeling than accomplishing something that others doubted you could. Our greatest leaders were doubted and now we follow in their footsteps of triumph...(3D)

May 31

The greatest gift you could ever give someone is showing them how to get back on their feet after they have fallen. Giving someone a helping hand will help them stand temporarily but showing them how to stand will help them anytime they fall. Don't give someone a temporary solution to a long time problem. That will only hurt them more in the long run because it will teach them to always look for temporary solutions. We tend to want to feel good for the day and worry about tomorrow when it comes but this turns tomorrow's issues into lifetime concerns. In order to feel joy tomorrow deal with your issues today...(3D)

Questions

1. What changes would you like to make to your present home or describe your future home?

2. Where would you like to live and why?

3. What famous restaurants or hotels would you like to visit if you don't know any describe your perfect vacation?

June

June 1

If given the opportunity to lead most would decline.
People love to have the title of leader because of the
glory it brings but they don't want the responsibility
that it carries with it. A leader must be willing to accept
all responsibility for the actions of its followers and be
willing to sacrifice themselves if things go wrong.
Leaders never point a finger at anyone unless they are
looking in the mirror. We must realize we are leaders to
people around us whether we want to be or not. A
leader who does not take responsibility for the actions
of his followers is the worst kind of leader with the
most unsuccessful followers…(3D)

June 2

Never take your aim off the target because once you do
you will lose sight of your dream. Negativity and
discouragement are sure-fire ways to miss your target.
When you allow these things to overshadow your
efforts you can't see where you're going. Being able to
see what's around the next bend allows you to move at
a faster pace because you can trust in your path and
abilities to succeed. Stay focused on your main
objective or your objective will become your main
disappointment…(3D)

115

June 3

When you look for love you are often hurt, but when you accept love you are often rewarded. You must have an open heart as well as an open eye because the heart can see things the eye cannot. The heart can lead you when it's too dark to see. The heart can show you a way when your eyes are clouded by tears. You can live without your eyes but you won't last a minute without your heart. Never put your eyes before your heart or you will be met with great disappointment when the view changes, and the view of the eyes changes frequently...(3D)

June 4

The difference between trust and faith is trust is something that you believe because it has been proven or can be proven to be true. Faith is believing something that you think is true but may not be able to be proven to be true. Faith is based on a feeling we have, rather than facts. We trust our cars to start when we turn the key and we have faith that we will arrive at our destination safely. Trust in your abilities and knowledge and have faith that your actions will deliver your dreams...(3D)

June 5

Energy cannot be created nor destroyed but it can be attracted and directed. If you feel like you don't have any energy left to achieve what you want then find a way to direct more energy to yourself. No one has a great impact on the world without the help of others either directly or indirectly. People have passed energy through time and space through recorded messages in books and other media. It's up to you to find sources of energy to help you keep pushing ahead. If you ever feel drained of energy, find a source to fill that void…(3D)

June 6

A second chance is not often given if the attempts the first time around were incorrect attempts. If you want something as much as you want to breath then you won't let opportunity pass you by. Don't allow your eyes to close because if you don't see a chance coming you won't be able to take advantage of it. When you are in full pursuit of a goal or dream you should not allow things like sleep get in the way. Our bodies are designed to last as long as we are active. Staying still weakens our muscles and mind, so act now and rest when the job is done…(3D)

June 7

Taking the time to truly understand will prevent premature actions and unnecessary feelings of regret. We are all subject to over reacting to the actions or words of people, but if we stop and think fully about why they said or did it, we might react differently. Fast actions sometimes lead to long regrets. Be careful of your reactions because you can't take back the past but you can alter the future….(3D)

June 8

Use your mind before your mouth. This will prevent you from having to apologize for things you may say that you do not mean. For all of us, our actions are a direct result of our thoughts. Some say they did not think before they did something, but that is not true. They simply did not think *enough* before acting. Do what you feel is right and you will be right 99% of the time. Do what you think is wrong and you will be wrong 99% of the time. Think more about the reactions of your actions and your decisions won't be mistakes…(3D)

June 9

To get to the top you must understand what it is like to be at the bottom. Lack of this understanding will result in less progression because you won't know how to avoid the things that separate the top from the bottom. There is nothing worse than a boss who does not relate to the issues of their employees. Understanding is caring and failure to care is the fastest way to fail in general…(3D)

June 10

Where there is effort there are results. Don't blame others for your shortcomings in life. Instead, use those shortcomings as opportunities to work harder. When you become content with your efforts, then the standards of what you have to do to feel satisfied become instantly higher. Being comfortable is the seed of laziness. Don't get caught up in just doing what is asked of you because you will receive minimum rewards. Perform always to your max and your rewards will soon be matched…(3D)

June 11

Pride builds confidence and confidence encourages faith. Be proud of who you are or make changes to your character so you can be proud of the person you will become. This self-pride helps your confidence rise like a helium balloon. You don't have to become the person you want to become over night, but every small step you make to become that person will make you feel proud. Too much pride will explode but with the right amount your confidence level will rise and you will soon be in the clouds of faith. Faith is so powerful it will get you through all hard times and will help you become victorious in all battles…(3D)

June 12

Accepting things you cannot change is the start to a productive and healthy life. No one picks their parents, birthplace, or time of birth. Those things just come to us the same way our appearance comes to us due to our genetic code. Focus on changing the things you can change like health and knowledge to free yourself from self-destruction. There is no point in chasing your dreams if you are not healthy enough to enjoy them when you attain them. Improve your health, if not for yourself then for the people who love you…(3D)

June 13

Stress causes the body to function improperly. Don't allow things that you cannot change to stress you. If you can change it do something about it right away. Stress has been known to stop life. Since stress is self-induced, it can be considered a form of suicide. Things always work out for the best when they are meant to. You cannot put a rush on fate but you can put a rush on faith…(3D)

June 14

A spider constructs a new web every night to catch a meal. Meanwhile, some people won't even look for a job to get a check. Pride is often the biggest roadblock on the path to achievement and it is only removed by the willingness to become humble. Those that allow this roadblock to remain on the path never see the end of the road and get trapped in their own web of short falls. They do not see that if they give up their pride, they will get something much better…(3D)

June 15

Don't accept failure as defeat. Look at it as practice for success. The person who has failed the most knows more about how to reach a particular goal than someone who has not even given it a shot. Learn from practice so that when you're in the actual game its second nature rather than a first attempt. Almost no one ever succeeds on their first attempt. It's usually not a problem with the game but a problem with the game plan. That's why there is a half time, so adjustments can be made to the game plan. Things change all the time as you play the game…(3D)

June 16

When a quitter decides to quit, they usually quit when they are closest to their goals. If it was meant to be easy then everyone would finish in 1st place and no effort would be required. Effort is like fuel to a fire: the more you put in, the greater the flame. When you stop putting fuel in, the flame dies and requires more fuel to restart it than it did to maintain it. Lack of effort will only result in lack of success. You can't succeed or fail if you never put in the work…(3D)

June 17

Everyone is born with expectations of success in life but with success comes great responsibility. Some people never seem to stop feeding from the bottle of life because it's much easier to suck then it is to chew. They don't want to put the effort in, they just want to get the nutrients out the easy way. They are the same people who feed off others and never give to anyone. Their eyes are closed and to the greater successes it could bring them because they are blinded by laziness...(3D)

June 18

If you ever want to change your status in life, change your priorities first. Adjusting the things you put emphasis on will adjust the results you get when you desire something. Priorities are the ingredients that go into reaching goals. You have to add them at the proper time and in the proper order or your dough won't rise. You must watch over them with a careful eye or your dreams will burn and become unreachable...(3D)

June 19

Parents and mentors often say, "Do as I say and not as I do." But in reality, we follow what our mentors do rather than what they say. People naturally follow by example so watch your actions more than you weigh your words—they speak louder....(3D)

June 20

Great success comes from great adversity. With every seed of disappointment grows a tree of victory with branches of triumph and leaves of accomplishments. Those leaves come and go as often as the seasons change, so make sure to enjoy them when they are present and remember what it was like to have them when the winter comes and times are hard. And remember, spring always follows winter no matter what happens…(3D)

June 21

Things that matter most are the things that weigh in your mind the heaviest. You can lighten your burdens of stress by removing people who add to your load. Real friends should be taking on some of your stress and carrying it on their shoulders. Everyone needs help but choosing the wrong people to get help from can be more burdensome than doing it alone.…(3D)

June 22

Changing small things in your day can have a large impact on your life. If you take the time to think about what you need to do differently then you have the time to just do it. It starts with a thought and should end with an action. If it does not end with action then there is no point in thinking about it. We are all subject to the consequences of our actions just as much as we are to the results of our non-action. If you want to see a change make a move towards that goal now…(3D)

June 23

Express gratitude to others around you often. You are where you are because of others and will get where you go because of others. All that you have done and accomplished is because of the people who helped build your character. Thank them for what they have done. Also, show gratitude for what you have because, while you may not think it is much now, within a split second it could be gone. You will never get more in life until you appreciate what you have now…(3D)

June 24

Love is something that comes with great reward but with every great reward there is great sacrifice. To truly feel what love can do you must be willing to give all of yourself and completely let go of ego or a fear of being vulnerable. The reward of giving all is getting all that love can bring. But, because there is such a great sacrifice involved, you must be careful of who and what you decide to love. Only love who or what you have faith to love you back. Your will should be greater than the gift because once you give all of yourself you will have nothing else left if the receiver is not worthy of the gift…(3D)

June 25

When dark days come and tears flow like running water remember that seeds require water to grow. Allow the tears that fall to be the beginning of new life. Put all you have into letting go. It's hard to get filled with joy when you are overflowing with sadness. Tears are a way to release sadness so you have more room for joy, so cry as often as you need. Just don't allow the water to be wasted. Plant good seeds in good soil and let the tears and sweat feed your seed…(3D)

June 26

It is better to die on your feet trying to accomplish something than to spend your entire life on your knees begging for something to happen. You must plan your course of action and put one foot in front of the other because it's much easier to get knocked down when you're standing still versus when you are moving. The cure to depression and feelings of defeat is constant motion. Constant motion will always end in forward movement...3D)

June 27

Watching TV strengthens the eyes and reading a book strengthens the mind. There are a lot of things you can learn from watching TV but the information is precooked. It's like putting dinner in the microwave; it will get the job done but won't taste the same or be as enjoyable as cooking it. Words on paper stimulate the mind and stimulate your imagination while pictures on the screen are the already-formed imagination of someone else and do not require your imagination to work....(3D)

June 28

Life is not about always looking for the greener grass. If you take care of your lawn properly and water it your grass will always be as green as the lawn on the other side. While we are looking for better we sometimes lose appreciation for what we have been blessed with. When you start looking on the other side make sure you take care of what you have first....(3D)

June 29

There is never a good reason to get even. The only thing getting even has ever done is cause more issues and add stress to one's life. Defense is meant to protect you from someone's offence, not to weaken someone's defense. It's not your job to get even because we are not here to judge nor enforce the sentence. Leave this responsibility to the high court of life and life will never put the responsibility in your hands…(3D)

June 30

Happiness is a state of being. Joy is a more immediate, intense feeling and is the result of being happy Find things in your life that make you happy so you can discover how to fill your heart with joy. Many people become happy while few ever experience joy because they allow negativity to overpower that feeling of happiness. Fight the darkness of tears with the light of laughter and you will soon be filled with the victory of joy….(3D)

Questions

1. What collectibles would you like to have in your collection?

2. What toys or luxuries would you like to have in your life, describe them?

3. What adventures would you like to go on?

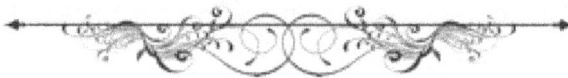

July

July 1

You never know if a small decision will turn into a life changing one, so make all decisions with clarity and an understanding of all the possible results. Failure to do so could result in the loss of things you value most. No one makes all the right choices all the time, but you can always think about your choices thoroughly. Don't rush to decide, but when you do decide stand firm with your choice. You came to it for a reason…(3D)

July 2

Opportunity comes to those who are patient but it leaves fast, so you must act fast to take advantage of the situation. The people you have never heard of are the ones who did not act swiftly. They assumed opportunity would wait for them, or come again. Opportunity waits for no one. You have to wait for and prepare for opportunity because it will leave as fast as it came…(3D)

July 3

Submission is a trait of champions. You have to totally submit to your cause if you want to get your desired results. Champions don't get their title by giving only a part of themselves. Championship requires a total commitment of self and submitting to the work required to get there. Like they say, "If you don't want to do the work then change your desires because nothing is given to those who don't give of themselves."...(3D)

July 4

A valley is an upside down mountain. In both, it takes more effort to reach the top than to get to the bottom, but the view from the top of a mountain is better than the view from the top of a valley. The top of a valley is just ground level. It simply means you have gotten yourself out of a negative situation. Meanwhile, the view from the top of a mountain is the clouds. It means you have reached success. You choose your view by deciding how high you want to climb...(3D)

July 5

Make a way for yourself by removing ignorance from your path. Never want something until you fully understand what you are asking for. Knowing what you want is the first step to finding the right route to take. Once you have chosen your route, prepare for turbulent storms. Once you begin to follow your dreams obstacles will form to impend your way....(3D)

July 6

Be a Shepard of men and not a sheep. Be a leader among your peers because your peers are influences to the world around them and can carry your message. People who feel they are leaders act more responsible than people who are being lead. Followers act foolishly when they are led by a fool—a leader who leads with no direction. In order to become a great leader, follow great leaders and avoid fools...(3D)

July 7

I don't know all the answers on how to get what you want out of life, but I can tell you this: doing nothing is a sure fire way not to attain them. Work to achieve small goals daily. This is how you will reach your dreams in life. No one can stop you from dreaming but many can slow your progression toward your dream. You allow people in your life and you can also keep them out...(3D)

July 8

Taking care of issues immediately is a true sign of a successful person. The longer you put small things off, the larger they become over time. When they are still small things they can be handled easier and quicker. The only thing waiting does is add more stress over a longer period of time. Stress is the reason that strong buildings fall and the reason some people can't get back on their feet...(3D)

July 9

Don't rely on others to fill your void of happiness. You never know what octane they will put in your tank. Even if they do offer you temporary happiness, when there is no one around you will not know how to pump your own gas—how to be happy on your own. You will be left stranded without a way out. Self-reliance is self-empowerment. The more you rely on others, the more power you give them over you and your ability to reach your goals. Find your inner strength and you will free yourself from needing others more than the healthy amount...(3D)

July 10

The strongest power is the power of thought. Thought can move people to move mountains. The joy you feel when you are in a good state of mind is the purest form of positive thought. Negative thoughts are just what they sound like—a minus. They detract from the positive. If you allow negative into your life you are taking away from your life. Stay positive and you'll stay alive...(3D)

July 11

We are often our own worst enemies in the battle for success. We allow things to prevent us from doing the things we know we should be doing. Instead, we do plenty of things we know will not help us reach our goals. No one is more responsible for our actions than ourselves, but we are often quick to place the blame. If we extended a thumb instead, we would see where most of the blame should be placed. Look inward before you blame outward...(3D)

July 12

Pain is the first line of defense against long-term issues. Pain is meant to warn us when something is wrong with our bodies and to bring attention to the area in need. It can be controlled with drugs because it is only in the mind. If you can control how you think you can control how you feel. When you allow others to hurt you mentally it affects the functions of the body. Don't let people cause pain in your life. Control pain by being mentally strong and spiritually healthy...(3D)

July 13

Everyone makes mistakes and has flaws because we are born into an imperfect world. The only part of our existence that is flawless lives in our dreams. Dreams are perfect so that we can have a standard to live our lives by and have something to motivate our actions. We can never reach perfection, but constantly striving for it will make you successful. The ability to forgive the mistakes of others is a test of our faith. The inability to forget is an imperfection. Follow your heart when the mind is lost between the flawless state of dreams and our imperfect world...(3D)

July 14

The secret of gaining true wisdom is not taking in all the information that you can. The secret is knowing how to filter out the useless information and only keep the useful information. Understanding the difference between the two is called knowledge. The more knowledge you gain, the easier it will become to retain true wisdom. Don't allow the negative in life to take up the much-needed space for positive. Focus on the things you want and allow the things you don't to remain in the shadows of unconscious thoughts...(3D)

July 15

Faith is taking the first step and not knowing where your foot will land, but believing it will land somewhere positive—somewhere that brings you closer to what you want. If you believe from the heart and have faith from the soul all things will end the way you would like them to. But the limitations of your faith will also limit the outcome of your desires. If you do not believe that you will be delivered what you ask for wholeheartedly, then you will get exactly that—only a part of a whole…(3D)

July 16

No man has ever been successful without the loving touch of a woman. Whether it be a mother, sister, or life partner, a woman provides a soft shoulder to cry on when everything seems hard. If a man is blessed to have both a partner and mother, then his reward in success will be twice as great. No man can stand straight without replacing the rib that is missing from birth…(3D)

July 17

It is one thing to be loved but a greater, more in-depth feeling to be told you are loved. Don't assume people know you love them just because you do things for them or you are there for them. Express love physically as much as you do verbally. Some people may miss the actions done for them out of love but no one can miss the words "I love you." Never assume someone knows you love them just because of what you do. At the same token, never assume someone loves you simply because they say it. Words and actions of love must complement each other…(3D)

July 18

The difference between a person who lives and one who is alive is the number of regrets they have in the end. A person who truly lives will usually have fewer regrets. They will have taken the chance to experience more even though they may have been afraid at the point. At the end of time, it becomes very apparent that there was no reason to ever fear, because death is certain. So you may as well try the things you want to try...(3D)

July 19

You must have courage to say you love someone because when you do this, you put your feelings out on a platter for others to take from. You feed them strength through your love. If you are loved you are empowered with strength to do things that others can only dream of. Those that take the chance to love are often hurt but the ones who never get hurt are also never loved. If you find the courage to love you will be rewarded with the strength that comes with being loved...(3D)

July 20

If there was an easy way to victory then we would never experience defeat. As long as you can breathe you can fight. The fight starts from within and that is why even when you are on your back you still can fight. Will power is stronger than any medicine that has ever been discovered. If will power can work to cure disease it can also be used to cure the disease of laziness—one of the main contributors to failure...(3D)

July 21

A burden divided is a burden you don't have to carry alone. Never assume your problem is larger than anyone else's. Everyone has pain and everyone has a bad day, week, or year at some point. For the strong ones, the sun still rises. See it through. If you can't find the strength within to see through your rough times, look for strength in others who are going through the same problems or have walked in the same shoes. The ones going through it can sympathize with you. The ones who have gone through it can advise you. Thinking you are the only one suffering shows a lack of humbleness and humility. The moment you open your mouth and share your struggles, you will find out you're not alone...(3D)

July 22

People tend to focus on how long you live but fail to realize what's truly important is how you live. A person who lives 20 full, adventurous years will feel they lived more than one who lived 100 dull ones. Recognize the worth of every single day by bringing meaning to it. Live as if it's your last day but have faith that tomorrow will come. Doing things because you don't have an expectation of the future affects your present and can cause you to make reckless decisions. But thinking you will live-forever can cause you to be stagnant. The present is a gift that you can enjoy now and the way you spend it can either enhance or harm your future...(3D)

July 23

If you know why you are living then it is not hard to find out how to live. Find a reason to be and seek 'til your eyes can no longer see. When you start seeing reasons, then others will soon know how important you are as well because of the actions you begin to take. The reason there is so much violence in society is because people don't realize how important they are. No one takes the time to tell people the world is a better place because they are there. You can change a person's *how* if you tell them *why*...(3D)

July 24

How much you value your life is apparent based on how much time you do or do not waste. Every second of every hour of everyday is just as important as the next. Don't spend your time on things that don't matter much, like relationships that you can't see going anywhere, or jobs you know you will not like forever. We don't know how much time we are given so make sure you spend time on the things that count. The difference between successful people and the ones that fail is successful people pursue their dreams while failures watch others obtain their dreams. Spend more time doing than watching...(3D)

July 25

Don't desire money, desire the things money may bring. Money is just a means to acquire the right tools to get things you want. If you just seek money then you won't know how to make the best of it when it's in your hands. Seek results and work backwards to discover how to get there, and how your money can be of use to you. It's much easier to break something down to see how it works than to have all the pieces and no instructions on how to put them together...(3D)

July 26

You can't expect people to know how to be in a committed relationship if they have never been exposed to one. We learn by example. We mature by adjusting these examples and adding to them. Maturity is not a natural thing. It is learned by doing, failing and learning from the downfalls. It is those learned lessons that make us grow spiritually and develop mentally...(3D)

July 27

Only accept and expect the best from people you love because if you settle for less than the love you have for yourself will be less. What you accept from others shows what you think you are worth. The less you think you are worth—the less you love yourself—the more you allow other people to take advantage of you. People can only do to you what you allow them to and false love makes fools of us all. While true love makes others want to *do* for you, not *want* from you...(3D)

July 28

It's hard to stand when the pressures of the world are on your shoulders but once you have pushed past that pressure and you're on your feet, it's harder to get knocked down again. If you never conquer difficult times you won't know what victory feels like and won't appreciate it when it's present in your life. Nobody starts a fight with plans to lose so why start your day with intentions to fail? Winning is a state of mind. It's not a trophy on the shelf...(3D)

July 29

The biggest difference between being at the top and the bottom is who is there with you. There will be plenty of people around you when you're doing great but when times are not good company is few and far between. The ones who are there to lift you when you are down and congratulate you when you're are on top are called friends. You will be able to see your true friends most clearly when times are tough. When you're at the top, you might be too blinded by the clouds of success to know who truly cares about you and who simply wants from you...(3D)

July 30

True power is the ability to move people emotionally. Being able to change how a person feels is the single most powerful gift. If you change a person's feelings then you can change their thoughts and changing people's thoughts is how you change the world. Find a person that you know is going through a hard time and put a smile on their face. You will see how your power to make them feel happy has changed their thoughts...(3D)

July 31

With great achievement comes great responsibility. Most people don't realize this. They think success is all about enjoying the good life for yourself, but when you are given the power of success it is your responsibility to help others who are less successful You will find that you won't even enjoy success very long if you do not use it to help others. If you want to be in a powerful position in life be prepared to give yourself to others, or your position will stay in constant jeopardy because people will be trying to take it from you... The best way to keep power is to share it and help others find their own power...(3D)

Questions

1. What is the best thing that has ever happen to you?

2. What is the most important thing ou learned in school?

3. What is your goal in life?

August

August 1

People never care much about anything tragic until it happens to them. If you start paying attention to issues that are affecting others you will have more time to prevent them from affecting you or a loved one. Never turn your back on things that are affecting other peoples lives because the second you think it could never happen to you, it does. Look at the situation of those struggling. Think of ways to help them. The methods you took to help them will be your own map to get you out of the same situation when it happens to you. A closed eye can't see the map so when you're lost you won't know how to get back...(3D)

August 2

The more you walk with lies the further you will fall from the truth. Lies only lead to more lies and more lies only lead to more people not wanting to be around you. When you think people don't realize you are living that is when you are living a lie, and living a lie is the quickest way to failure. It's like building a house made of cardboard, it works well until it rains...(3D)

August 3

People spend their entire lives trying to find that person they relate to so they can create a relationship but most miss the most important part of building a relationship with someone else, which is building a healthy relationship with yourself first. Mold your own personality to be one that is inviting, friendly, welcoming, and warm yet independent. When you have all the traits yourself that you are looking for in another person, your choice in relationships will soon become numerous…(3D)

August 4

Giving from the heart feeds your soul. It's an emptiness that is never quite filled because there's always more you can give and there are always people who are in need. If we were all given the same things and opportunities from the beginning then there would not be any chance to test a person's willingness to give. That is why the more one is given, the more they are expected to give...(3D)

August 5

To overcome a loss or adversity is to gain a victory. If you want to be a winner spend more time getting up and even a greater amount of time learning how to stand. It is easy to fall down when you are grounded in the soft soil of materialism and greed and it is easy to get up and stand when your foundation is based on faith and sacrifice...(3D)

August 6

As you walk down the long road of life you never know where it will lead. Walk each step with desire as your motivation and dreams will create bridges to connect where you are to where you want to be. Always remember where your journey began but never lose site of the right means to get to the end...(3D)

August 7

All good things must come to an end and so do the bad ones. Don't make someone else your entire world because when they are gone you will have nothing. If you put your faith in your self and believe you can achieve anything you will never allow trenches of failure to become valleys of defeat. Instead you will be able to turn hills of success into mountains of triumph. Only you can stop you so don't let others hinder what you dream to do...(3D)

August 8

You are an influence to others whether you want to be or not. Watch what you say and do because someone is always watching you. Think about it, you are the product of the people who raised you and the environments that you were brought up in. You became what you are by watching others. You don't have to become the people you see but you have to see the person you have become. Be a role model not a model who plays a role...(3D)

August 9

Don't allow discouragement to take hold of your thoughts. When you feel it's the worst time and the journey seems like it's at its hardest climb that means you are closer than you have ever been to reaching your goals. Success is predictable because it always follows failure. But you have to keep your eye on the prize and never allow the seed of doubt to be planted...(3D)

August 10

When times seem like they are hard, it's because they are. When it seems like it is the worst it can be, it probably is. But there is only one direction to go from rock bottom, and that is up. When you are going through rough times, keep in mind it's so that when you're at the top looking down on someone who is going through them, you can be their light at the end of life's dark tunnels. It's easy to stand once someone teaches you how...(3D)

August 11

Basing a relationship off looks is like buying a house because of the color of the paint. With age it will fade and will not look as it did in the beginning, and long before then you might discover the foundation is very weak. A relationship should be based on communication as the foundation and understanding as the walls that hold up the roof of respect. When bad weather comes you need to have these things in place. These are what make up what we call "home" and you want your relationship to be something you are happy to "come home to" during hard times...(3D)

August 12

Saying you will "try" something is like preparing to fail. The more you only "try" the closer you get to failure. If you are taking the time to think about trying then you are not spending your time doing. To try is to have an excuse why you did not accomplish a set goal. You can always say, "I tried...". You did not accomplish it because you were trying. It takes a lot less effort to do than it does to try. If you're constantly saying you tried, that means you did not work hard enough...(3D)

August 13

If you can accomplish goals during a time when life is dealing you hard cards, you learn endurance. Once you learn to endure you realize all negative things in life will pass. All days may not be bright but you can make light of all dark ones. Learning to turn negative into positive is learning how to take control of your life. Once you are in control, no one can change your path...(3D)

August 14

Negativity is often a wolf dressed in sheep's clothes. Be careful of the gifts you receive. The giver might seem like they have kind intentions, but they are actually giving to get something in return. If you do something for someone but complain about having done it later then you did not have pure intentions. Do not give with the intention of getting something in return. That isn't called giving. That is called an investment...(3D)

August 15

Life waits on no one so you should never wait on life. You have to learn how to make things happen for yourself. Asking others for help, before learning how to help yourself, only prolongs failure because you won't know how to progress on your own. Giving to someone who is looking for a hand out only teaches him or her to reach their hand out further. Put a hammer in that hand and supply them with wood and nails and they will never have to worry about a roof over their heads. Give them the tools to help themselves, rather than the help...(3D

August 16

You can't find something until you learn to recognize it so love will only find you once you learn to love yourself. The more you care about yourself, the more you will learn to care for others. Trying to love another person who you know does not love you is another form of not loving yourself. Do not constantly give of yourself to a person who does not want to give back to you. Never allow the love you want to have for another to overshadow the love you have for yourself and family....(3D)

August 17

Lives that are made of superficial straw are often blown down by the big bad wolf of life. We need to learn how to build our lives with humble bricks and mortar to withstand all the negative and painful times we will endure. Failure to appreciate and remember the work and effort it takes to build a solid life will result in constant reconstruction. It's easier to knock a house down than it is to build it up...(3D)

August 18

Don't allow the influences of others steer you away from your chosen path. Friends who truly want to help will only offer motivation and inspiration. A positive influence is obvious but a negative influence can come in many different forms, such as an enemy masquerading as a friend...(3D)

August 19

The person you are in a relationship with should also be your best friend. This should be the person that has your back when the rest of the world seems against you, the person you can tell anything too, and the person that makes your life complete. You can't be successful by yourself. It takes a best friend and a strong relationship to help lift you from the valleys, and to enhance your feelings of joy when you share them with them...(3D)

August 20

If you are searching for your purpose in life you can always be certain you are on the right track by helping someone in need. Help someone who does not ask for it. Give to someone in need who will not admit they are in need. Do something for someone who is always doing for others. Our purpose is not to be rich and famous. Rather, the purpose of being rich and famous is to help others who are not...(3D)

August 21

Willingness to render humble service will fill your heart and mind, but not your pocket. Seek out things you can do for others that will not render you the reward of money. The rewards are greater for free service because no amount of money can bring you joy like the appreciation of another person can. You can't buy your way to heaven but you can work your way into a more favorable situation...(3D)

August 22

Attitudes are contagious. When you have a positive attitude the people around you will also display positive attitudes, because you will give them no reason to have bad ones. Having a bad attitude is like the bad apple in a bunch of good ones. If you wonder why things aren't going well in your life consider what your outlook on life has been. To change the people around you and the events that take place start with yourself and your attitude. Others will follow your lead...(3D)

August 23

When you work, do more than what is asked of you. If you get in the habit of doing more than what is required, you will receive larger rewards than you expected. Even if the work is for yourself, the more effort you put into it, the more you will appreciate what people do for you and the work they put into helping mold your character...(3D)

August 24

Trust is the lubricant that helps all parts of a relationship move more smoothly, like oil in a car. Without it, the car can't move. When low, you can move forward but it takes more effort and you might burn your engine out. Check your oil and top it off everyday. It takes a lot more to refill a tank once it is empty, and it takes much more effort to rebuild a relationship once it has completely fallen apart…(3D)

August 25

There is no greater joy than the joy of laughter. Find a reason to laugh everyday and you will find a reason to live everyday. Laughter makes even the most negative situations more bearable. Laughing helps heal the mind body and soul. When you laugh it uplifts your spirit and the spirits of the people around you. When you are feeling down, laugh at yourself and your situation. There is nothing wrong with that. It is an indicator that you will push through. Just let the stress go and laugh your cares away...(3D)

August 26

Love is never meant to hurt. If it hurts, it's not true love. Love means sacrifice and since it's not easy to sacrifice, it's not easy to love. But, when you truly love someone, sacrificing for them should not be painful. Love is a pure and true emotion that changes people's lives and the world if used correctly. If you think you are loved or that you love someone but that love brings pain, it's not love. It's confusing. You will know the difference when you are truly in love. So don't settle for anything less, just because you haven't experienced the best yet...(3D)

August 27

Falling down is easy. It does not require any assistance and is usually the result of failure to plan correctly. Usually, you know why you are going to fall before you fall. Getting up is a test of faith. Getting up requires that you remember how to stand. If you don't remember that, then getting up is useless. Standing is the hardest part of life. When you are standing, you can see all those who have fallen and you feel the responsibility to help them…(3D)

August 28

Demand things you want in life. But don't expect them to come overnight. Don't spend your time fulfilling the dreams and desires of other people before your own. Look out for yourself first. You need to have experienced happiness yourself before you will even have the energy to help others find it. Once you own happiness and feel true love you can teach others how to get to that point as well…(3D)

August 29

The only difference between a dream and reality is your level of faith. When you dream, you create your own reality and anything is possible. It is only when others tell you something is impossible, and you believe them, that your dreams fade and become memories. Don't let others kill your dreams because they have lost their faith and belief. Just because they did not reach theirs doesn't mean you can't reach yours. Although, they might tell you that is the case. Dream often and follow your faith in pursuit of your dreams. In the pursuit of happiness you realize your dreams…(3D)

August 30

People always mistake their wants for needs and for that reason speak about those wants constantly. The more you tell people what you want the less they are inclined to respond. No one is attracted to someone who is desperate for something. People are attracted to others who are self-confident and seem to have it all. Stop telling people what you want and start acting like you already have it. It will come to you much faster and in a higher quality…(3D)

August 31

There is a big difference between being still and doing nothing. Sometimes we all need to just stop and be still for a while. We need to look around and take it all in. Being still allows you to hear and not be heard, see and not be seen, know and not be known. If you want to make a difference, you have to know what's really going on before you can do something about it...(3D)

Questions

1. What does success mean to you?

2. What brings you the most joy in life right now?

3. What one thing you accomplished are you most proud of?

September

September 1

People always talk about being afraid to die. But dying is the result of being born. Don't fear something that has to happen and is going to happen no matter what. That fear requires energy, and that energy is just wasted. Focus more on not being afraid to live. Most people, while fearing the end of life, forget to live. Live as if life is a gift and be grateful for all of the rewards it brings everyday...(3D)

September 2

Be careful of the company you keep. Consider your friends a mirror, because we are judged by the company we keep. They are a reflection of you, so if you are talking about them in a negative way you are really talking poorly about yourself. It's a real example of "two birds of the same feather." If you are a dove who hangs around crows, you'll be judged as a crow. And all of your beautiful dove-like qualities will be overshadowed by the dark crow. In the end, all of you will become unwanted company...(3D)

September 3

Follow your heart but let your mind guide you in the right direction. Fools do foolish things and allowing emotions to lead you would be foolish. Emotions are temporary and thoughts can last forever so think constantly about the ones you love and care for. When those loved ones are gone, you will have the memories of the things you did together, and of their character, and that thought of emotion will last you forever...(3D)

September 4

If you let the small set backs in life get you down there is no way you will be able to handle the major ones. Sometimes taking one small step backwards allows you to see the next few steps forward clearly. The future will seem cloudy if your path is not grounded in faith, and if you don't use your past as a tool for education. We would not be who we are if we did not learn from what we have done...(3D)

September 5

All great leaders have followed the lead of another great leader. To be successful you have to model yourself after successful people. Most things we want in life, we will find someone else has already achieved them. But that is a good thing, it gives us a model to follow, and one we can improve on. It would be foolish not to do some of the same things the model did to get their desired results. Take what you learn and add to it to create your own path to success...(3D)

September 6

Look around and realize how important the people around you are. If you don't feel they are important, then why have them around? Surround yourself with those that care about your well-being and your success. It's important to be selfish sometimes because thinking about yourself first make others realize how important you really are to them. Not being at their beck and call makes them realize how much value you were to them....(3D)

September 7

Time is something we cannot gain more of but lose every second. It is the greatest gift we have been given. Regrets are a waste of time because they are things we did or did not do with the gift we were given, but that particular gift,—that particular moment in time—is gone, so there is no point in thinking about how it could be used differently. Use your gift of time with the ones you love and the ones who love you. When the gift of time is no more, regret soon overwhelms those that are left to endure...(3D)

September 8

(L.O.V.E.): Living to overcome varied emotions...that you have toward someone you care deeply about. It's all about the ups and downs in a relationship. It's that thing that will pull you back up when you are down—the thing that makes you do things you would not normally do. So love yourself first and another will soon love you...(3D)

September 9

Allow persistence to get you through all doubt. Use determination to lift you from all valleys. Use desire to keep you going when times are tough. Use dreams to give you purpose in life. Use the faith in your heart as a light to guide you through the dark days. Happiness cannot be found in others and is a place you must find within yourself...(3D)

September 10

If you spend all of your time looking for the right person, you might find yourself very lonely. But if you settle for less then what you want, you will find your self unhappy. You must make the decision to have the strength to be alone until the right person comes into your life. If you fill up that place with the wrong person, just because you are lonely, then you won't see the right person when you meet him...(3D)

September 11

Don't use the word "try" when you want to succeed. Ask to succeed. Demand success. By saying you are trying, that means you are attempting to do something with the possibility of failure on the forefront of your brain. It means you are not visualizing success. Those who are visualizing it say they are "doing." Success will come when there is no other option. Trying leaves room for failure, especially if you are not trying hard enough...(3D)

September 12

No one can do it alone. Everyone who has achieved great things was motivated and supported by a partner or lover. To achieve greatness, you must have the support of the people you surround yourself with. The greatest and most influential people in your life are the ones who you are the closest to, like your best friend or lover. If you are with someone who is not supportive, it will hinder you form reaching your dreams...(3D)

September 13

Stress is one of the leading causes of heart problems. Our heart is one of the things in our bodies that reacts very strongly to the thoughts we have in our minds. Some thoughts we cannot control, like instincts, but others we can control, like feelings. Get rid of things and people that cause stress in your life. If you don't let other people control your thoughts, you prevent them from controlling your heart....(3D)

September 14

Dreams give you the opportunity to do all the things you want to do. When you pair determination with desire and persistence you can make your dreams turn into reality. Don't listen to the people who tell you that you can't attain your dreams. Those are the people who don't dream and settle for what they get in life...(3D)

September 15

Indecision is the main cause of failure. Indecision turns into doubt and when you mix the seed of indecision with the water of doubt, you develop a strong sense of fear. When you make a decision, have faith that your choice is the right one and stick to it. This will remove all sense of doubt and help you master your fears...(3D)

September 16

A true champion is the one who has faith in the time and practice they put towards their goals—faith that it will pay off when it's time to perform. So much faith that they try to get the ball in the last seconds of the game. They have faith they will come through with the victory. That is champion faith and it will not accept defeat, but actually accelerates furthest when it is close to defeat...(3D)

September 17

Cleansing the body out has become very popular. Juice cleansing, colon cleansing, master cleansing etc... People do this to get rid of extra weight and toxins in the body, but many forget to do mental cleansing. There are a lot of toxins and added weight in our minds, so don't forget to mental cleanse for a better quality of life...(3D)

September 18

Positive and negative thoughts can't be in your mind at the same time. You have to decide what thoughts you want to have and when. Why not always have positive thoughts? You can. You just have to do something different to change the way you are thinking when you have negative ones. Life is too short to be negative towards anything. Think positive and positive things will happen to you....(3D)

September 19

People will show up when things are going great in your life, but few will be there when things are going poorly. When you're not doing well, take time to reflect and pay attention to who is actually still there for you. That way, when you get back on your feet, you can appreciate the ones who helped pick you up...(3D)

September 20

Use every setback and downfall as a new rung in the ladder of success. Every step you take on the path to success creates a path for others to follow. They say it's lonely at the top, and this could be true because few people have the stamina to push forward when the climb becomes tough and the air gets thinner. So there will be fewer people at the top, but they will be of high quality....(3D)

September 21

Ask yourself where you want to be and what you want to be doing in the next 5 years. Write it down and read it. Ask yourself if you really want it. Make plans and steps to get to that point. Only surround yourself with people that want you to succeed and will help you get to that point. After you get there, be thankful for the roller coaster ride it took to reach that point called happiness...(3D)

September 22

Successful people take care of their bodies. Eat right and exercise. Even if not for yourself, do it for the ones who care about you. You're here because of those who came before you, and they had the pleasure of sticking around to know you because they took care of their bodies. So, if you want to be around for a long time for those who depend on you and enjoy your company, think before you eat...(3D)

September 23

Don't be careful of what you ask for, just demand what you really want. Getting what you really want in life can never be a bad thing, so long as you know you really want it. You can't make a mistake when you follow your heart. You only make mistakes when you make decisions based on emotions because when that emotion has passed, the decision has already been made and the repercussions of it will not leave with the emotion...(3D)

September 24

If you continue to settle for less you will never gain more. Never let anyone convince you that you should accept something you don't want. Whether it be a job, relationship, car, or whatever it may be. At the end of the day, it is always easier to have someone kick you than attempt to kick yourself for something you know you should not have done...(3D)

September 25

It's your actions, not your words, that count. It takes a lot of courage to act on a decision and stick by your choice than it does to talk about it...(3D)

September 26

The mark of genuine wisdom is modesty and silence. Talk less and listen more and the wiser you will become....(3D)

September 27

We rise to high positions or remain at the bottom because of how we manage the conditions we actually have control over. But this only happens if we desire to control them. Know what you want and go for it. You can control the outcome if you are willing to sacrifice (have love) for that desire...(3D)

September 28

Friends are ones who, no matter what, tell you things with the intention of helping you. Sometimes, their words may hurt but that probably means they are telling the truth. Friends are the ones who care more about your well being than whether or not they offend you...(3D)

September 29

Sometimes you try to do what's best for yourself and later you find out it was not the best for you. But you can't see your shadow if your head is toward the sun. Think about what was done wrong and do what you know now is right. Always look up and ahead and let what's behind you push you forward...(3D)

September 30

The word "relationship" stems from the idea of how well you relate to those in the same ship as you. Think about it: if you were going to take a long trip across the ocean, with limited water, food and room, who would you take with you? You would choose people you know you can relate to on your ship. So, why would you be in a relationship with someone you would not put on your ship?...(3D)

September 31

They say, "Be careful what you ask for because you just might get it, but if you don't ask for it you will never get it." You must demand what you want in life. Write it down, recite it, believe it. You can have whatever you like. But a closed mouth causes starvation...(3D

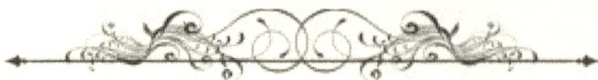

Questions

1. What makes you happy?

2. What do you enjoy most?

3. Who do you admire most and why?

October

October 1

What is love? Love is sacrifice. The greatest love of all time was indicated with a cross for the sign of the ultimate sacrifice. If you question your love for another or theirs for you, ask yourself what you would be willing to sacrifice for them, or what you think they would be willing to sacrifice for you. Your level of willingness to sacrifice is an indicator of your level of love....(3D)

October 2

Happiness is not a thing you can hold. It is a state of being. Find out what truly makes you happy and pursue it. In the end, the only thing you will leave behind is how you make people feel, and if you make yourself happy, you will make others happy. Live to be happy. Don't live to get things you think will make you happy eventually....(3D)

October 3

Indecision is one of the main causes of failure. Do not rush to make a decision before thinking it through, but once you have thought about all of the sides of the situation make your decision. Change decisions slowly and not often. Your instincts exist for a reason. Follow them and you're going to be right 90% of the time...(3D)

October 4

Our actions and conduct make us who we are. We create the individual that we see when we look in the mirror; it is completely within our control. If you want to change how people view you, you must change how you view yourself by changing the way you behave...(3D)

October 5

It is said that life is full of pot holes and speed bumps, so make sure you have great shocks on your vehicle. Those shocks are the friends, family and the company you keep. If you forget about the ones who care about you, the road will become bumpy very quickly....(3D)

October 6

Sometimes when we are planning the future we have to look in the past and see what we need to change. If you don't change your actions based on the mistakes you have made in the past, then history will repeat itself. To change what's ahead, start with analyzing what is behind....(3D)

October 7

It isn't the lawyer with the best knowledge about the law who wins; it's the one who best prepares his case. Proper preparation prevents poor performance....(3D)

October 8

A manager is someone who does things right. A leader is someone who does the right thing. Manage things right, and one day you might just turn around and realize that someone is following you. That is the day you become a leader, and must also concern yourself with doing the right thing...(3D)

October 9

Don't just keep trying the same old thing expecting different results. Take a look from the outside in and you might not like what you see. Sometimes we are clouded by our own egos and pride. That is the same ego and pride that will prevent us from getting what we really want, which is to be happy...(3D)

October 10

The greatest thing that anyone can do is be a servant of people. By serving others you do a service to yourself and not only is that good for your heart, it is good for your soul. It is always better to give, because that is the action that will ensure you will receive...(3D)

October 11

Practically all great fortunes come from selling services or selling ideas. That means our true fortunes are already in us and it's up to us to figure out how to offer them to the world...(3D)

October 12

Temporary defeat is a sign that something is wrong with the plan. You have to perfect the plan in order to realize the goal. You can only be defeated if you decide not to change the plan and accept it for what it is...(3D)

October 13

No individual has enough experience, education, natural ability and knowledge to ensure the accumulation of great fortune without the cooperation of other people....(3D)

October 14

Give life, action and guidance to your ideas and they will take on a power of their own and you will see all opposition sweep away. Your ideas have the power to live longer than the brain that created them, so don't let your ideas go to waste. Put them to work for you now....(3D)

October 15

Ideas are products of the imagination. The simpler and easily adaptable an idea is, the greater value it has. Sometimes less is truly more...(3D)

October 16

Imagination means capability. Imagination is the one quality needed to combine specialized knowledge with ideas to create organized plans that will yield desired results. Dream to see what others can imagine....(3D)

October 17

Educated people don't have all the knowledge, they just know where to get the information (knowledge) when they need it and know how to organize it into definite plans of action. Educate yourself about what you want to attain the things you want....(3D)

October 18

People are always quick to tell you what "they" say you should do, and the way "they" say to get there. But if you spend your time listening to "them" you will find yourself just like the "they"—not unique, but one in a bunch...(3D)

October 19

You get tired much faster chasing your own dreams than you do chasing someone else's. And that is because you don't work as hard chasing someone else's dreams, because they aren't worth the effort to you. But the results feel better in the end when you chase your own dreams. When you are working for someone else you are helping them reach a goal but what goals are you setting for yourself to reach?...(3D)

October 20

The only way to attain your true desire is to see it, taste it, touch it and smell it before you have it. Feel as if you already have it and demand it! Push yourself to attain it and don't let anyone or anything stand before you. Only keep those who believe in you and who will push you around you....(3D)

October 21

The reason you can become the master of yourself and of your environment, is because you have the power to influence your own subconscious mind. Think it and believe what you think to achieve what you believe!!...(3D)

October 22

Faith removes all the limitations of your thoughts. Have faith and soon success will follow faith's lead...(3D)

October 23

Thoughts are magnets that attract similar thoughts; when mixed with emotion and planted as a seed in faith, they help you receive your desires...(3D)

October 24

Faith is the only known antidote for failure. Believe in yourself and your abilities—show that you feel successful in your actions and words—and no one will ever think you have ever failed....(3D)

October 25

History is full of great thinkers but history only remembers great doers. Act on your thoughts and be recognized. If you only think, you will never be recognized for those ideas...(3D)

October 26

When you combine faith (the fuel) with desire (the rocket) you reach your dreams (the stars)..... Reach high and think positive!!!!...(3D)

October 27

You must have faith in your ability to succeed. Faith is the "eternal elixir" that gives life, power, and action to the impulse of thought...(3D)

October 28

When your mind is dominated by positive emotions, those emotions will encourage you to feel faith. If you don't have faith, then fate will have you...(3D)

October 29

You must have that desire which recognizes no such word as "impossible," and accept no such reality as failure to reach where you want to be in life...(3D)

October 30

Stand up and be recognized. Don't sit down, blend in, and be overlooked. Demand great things to happen to you and don't accept anything less, because if you accept less, that's exactly what you will get...(3D)

October 31

It is a lot better to challenge yourself and challenge your limits, even if you do not succeed all the time. Living without challenges means you won't know defeat or victory. And living without ever knowing either of those is not truly living....(3D)

Questions

1. What are you most thankful for?

2. What is your most memorable experience and why?

3. What have you been avoiding that needs to be done?

November

November 1

Even the people who you never heard of had desire for great things. They are simply the ones who allowed one little failure to feel like complete defeat....(3D)

November 2

 Everything of value in civilization is a result of dreams. Without dreams, there would be no plans and without plans there would be no execution. Use your dreams as tools to reach your goals...(3D)

November 3

Use "desire" as a road map to achieving an overall career objective and more short-term "goals" as stepping stones along the way....(3D)

November 4

Persistence that does not recognize failure will bring success and riches. If you do not accept setbacks as failure, but rather recognize them as simple bumps on your road to success and even learning experiences, you will always reach success....(3D)

November 5

Burning desire means wanting something more than anything else. Leave yourself with no other options other than success and you will get what you desire—success. If you desire it you can acquire it...(3D)

November 6

Desire means knowing clearly what you want in life. Desire what you want to accomplish, have faith in your ability to do it and then pursue it until you have accomplished your goals...(3D)

November 7

If you truly desire something, say money, then become (money) conscious until the desire for (money) drives you to create a definite plan for acquiring it...Fill in the () with whatever you like, and focus on it in everything you do. You will eventually have no choice but to work towards it...(3D)

November 8

Success comes to those who become conscious of success. You must think about success and nothing else to achieve success and nothing else...(3D)

November 9

Failures are practice shots. The more you make them, the better you will perform when it's game time...(3D)

November 10

If you make time for yourself then the time you spend with others will be more enjoyable. You must discover all the things about yourself before you can understand other people. To try and understand why people do the things they do ask yourself first why you do the things that you do. It is not the *what* but the *way* someone does something. That is where true meaning is found. Search within to understand what's outside. Criticize yourself before you attempt to criticize others and you will find that most people have the same faults. The difference between people is how they turn faults into assets and weakness into strength and this is only done through understanding…(3D)

November 11

When you are truly ready for a thing, it puts itself in your presence. But it doesn't put itself there even one second before you are ready to receive it…. (3D)

November 12

It's so hard to listen to directions when you are telling others where to go. Sometimes it pays to listen; you will be amazed at what you hear...(3D)

November 13

Real wealth cannot be measured by what you have, but by what you are and how you affect the people around you. You are what people think you are...(3D)

November 14

A person who knows what they want in life has already gone a long way towards achieving it. The biggest step towards getting what you want is identifying exactly what it is. Once you really know what it is you want, you can start the process of attaining it, and no step taken after that will be a waste of time...(3D)

November 15

Great achievement is usually born out of great sacrifice, and is never the result of selfishness. Think of others if you would like to be thought of yourself...(3D)

November 16

Never expect negative things to happen; they have a tendency to show up when invited. You can never win if you expect to lose...(3D)

November 17

Success requires no explanations. Meanwhile, failure permits no alibis. Succeed more to become successful and fail often if you never want to be defeated....(3D)

November 18

More gold has been mined form the thoughts of men than has ever been taken from the earth. The greatest innovations and improvements in life came from thoughts before anything else. Since we put value on things, if your thoughts were things what would they be worth?...(3D)

November 19

The ladder of success is never crowded at the top, that is because determination is heavy and is hard for most to carry with them on the way up.........(3D)

November 20

No one achieves great success that is unwilling to make personal sacrifices. You must be willing to give of yourself to gain in the eyes of others. Nothing comes easy because sacrifice is not easy....(3D)

November 21

Conceit is a fog that will envelop your real character beyond your own recognition. It will weaken your native ability and strengthen all your faults. Be proud but not conceited.....(3D)

November 22

Everything in life starts out small as a seed and requires nutrients to make it develop into its full potential. Sometimes when we have ambitious goals we overlook the very first step because we are focusing on the results. We spend all of our time focusing on the effects without thinking about the cause. To reach the full potential of a goal, we need to focus on the seed and what it is going to take for that seed to sprout into its full potential. Everything that ends big starts small....(3D)

November 23

Success and failure are largely the result of habit. Think about your habits and change what you do to get the different results you want...(3D)

November 24

Every adversity, every failure, and every heartache carries with it the seed of an equal or a greater benefit. What kind of soil are you planting your seed in?....(3D)

November 25

Success comes to those who are success conscious and failure comes to those who allow themselves to become failure conscious. This means they are ultra aware of every failure, and they are unable to move on from it or stop thinking about it. Don't accept what you are given. Become aware of what you want and understand how to get there...(3D)

November 26

Both poverty and riches, success and failure, are offsprings of thought. Change your thoughts and you change your reality...(3D)

November 27

You can't teach a person to see but you can show them how to open their eyes....(3D)

November 28

We are separated from animal because of our unique ability to control our animal instincts and create our own patterns. Why accept things the way they are if you have the power to change them?......(3D)

November 29

Your mental attitude is something you control fully. You must use self discipline to create thought patterns, which keep your mental attitude positive at all times. If you want to attract positive things to you, think positive...(3D)

November 30

There are 2 kinds of people in the world: those which will not do what they are told, and those that do nothing else. You have to find a way to be a little of both or you will find yourself just another number to be counted......(3D)

Questions

1. What can you do to improve your mood everyday?

2. What do you spend most of your free time doing? Is it helping you accomplish a goal in anyway?

3. If you kne
w today was your last day on earth what is the first thing you would do?

December

December 1

Nothing can be called failure until you accept it as such. Don't accept what you don't want. Pursue your desire with unwavering determination. Allow what you want to overwhelm you with faith...(3D)

December 2

Someone once said, "Knowledge is power!" But this is only half true. Knowledge is power only when it is put into action for a definite objective...(3D)

December 3

That which you do to or for another person, you instantly do to and for yourself. People who do things just for themselves find that others around them will follow and do the same....(3D)

December 4

Taking the path of least resistance makes all rivers and some men to run crooked. It is a lot easier to do things that are not right because there are no expectations attached to the wrong. The more you do the wrong thing, the fewer expectations people have on you and the less pressure you feel. Doing the right thing brings with it the burden of responsibility...(3D)

December 5

It is more profitable to be a good listener than a good talker because one is always inclined to learn something while listening to others, but never learns anything form hearing oneself talk.....(3D)

December 6

Believe and you shall receive. Use faith as your guide. You are only limited by your own mental capacity to believe....(3D)

December 7

People should just help sometimes and not expect or ask for anything in return. The ones that do ask for something in return are really just thinking about themselves, and the quality of the favor they do for others is determined only by how much they believe people will do something in return for them...(3D)

December 8

Whatever the mind can conceive and believe, you can achieve. Allow your heart to be a beacon of light that guides your faith to your goals...(3D)

December 9

Your only real limitation is the one you set up and accept in your own mind. There is no external force that can actually completely limit you. You can jail a man and take away his freedom but you can never jail the mind. If a door ever closes on a situation or opportunity, you always hold the key to your freedom—it is in your thought...(3D)

December 10

No more effort is required in order to aim high to demand abundance and prosperity than is required to demand misery and poverty. Use your effort for the things you want in life and don't give light to the things you don't...(3D)

December 11

Closed minds will not inspire faith, courage or belief. Closed minds shut positivity out and allow doubt in, and doubt is the killer of all dreams and desires...(3D)

December 12

Wake up this morning, look in the mirror and say, "I am special!" Don't depend on others to tell you what you already know. Self motivation is found within yourself...(3D)

December 13

An expert is a person who has made all the mistakes that can be made in a very narrow field. You must fail often to succeed once...(3D)

December 14

Dig deep for our roots, our souls, the truth. To become grounded today we need to know what got us here. We can't stand firm if we're in quicksand. The economy is bad, but this is the time we need to dig deep and look for new ways of doing things new ways of making money. That's innovation through realization...(3D)

December 15

Even if it's a long way off, someone has to dream it before anyone can do it. Someone has to think it before someone can dream it. It's up to you if you want to do it 3D

December 16

Fail often to succeed sooner. Failure is proof that you took a risk, and if you don't take risks the odds are you won't succeed...(3D)

December 17

Living a quality life allows the lessons you learn to have a lasting effect. You never know who benefits from your life, and the ones who benefit sometimes don't realize who is the benefactor but the result of your actions in life remain the same....(3D)

December 18

Life is a temporary assignment. Live it to the fullest and remember your relationships are the most important thing you can have. Treat them as such and give them the time they need to grow. Nothing happens overnight and nothing lasts longer than a relationship that you develop....(3D)

December 19

Feel like a lion right now. Feel like a king. Feel like you can't be stopped. Once you learn what your weaknesses are, you develop them into strengths. So once someone thinks they have you figured out, you switch the game up...(3D)

December 20

They say if you think long you think wrong, but that does not mean if you think fast you think right. Take your time and make good decisions because you never know how far the impact of your decisions will travel...(3D)

December 21

It's always about the star player. When the economy is down and bad and you only have time and money to invest in one thing, invest in the star player (yourself). It's the only way to achieve success...(3D)

December 22

All of man's labor is for his stomach, yet his appetite is never satisfied. We are the only creatures who hunger for more than food. We have desires and emotions that bring more satisfaction than any meal. Don't spend all your time working for the stomach, work for the mind...(3D)

December 23

Things only change if you make them change. Put in the effort and you will soon see the results you want. If you don't see the desired results, change how you're going about getting there. There is nothing that changes on its own other than time and by using time as an asset you strengthen your skill of patience...(3D)

December 24

Energy cannot be created or destroyed, so you must take all negative energy and change it into positive. You cannot get rid of energy so cultivate it into the energy you desire. The more you practice, the easier it becomes...(3D)

December 25

The harder you push, the harder they push back. No one can achieve without receiving resistance. If it were easy, then no one would ever fail. It's about how you stand up once you're knocked down. Those that don't get back up never achieve...(3D)

December 26

Be thankful for Monday. It's funny how everybody can't wait until Friday. It's like you don't care about the rest of the week. If you live your life in happiness, everyday will be like Friday and the weekend will be like Monday...(3D)

December 27

At some point in your life, you must decide whether you want to impress people or influence people. You can impress people from a distance, but you must get close to influence them. When you do that, they will be able to see your flaws. Exposing your flaws is a way of building trust of the ones you want to influence...(3D)

December 28

Innovation through realization is the only true way to monetization, so long as your spending is moderate. Take anything and think for a second how it could be better (a product, a book, a movie even your life). That is called imagination. Imagination is the only thing that can't be taken away but it can be hindered if not used daily...(3D)

December 29

True realization comes only through reflection. Take the time for "me time." You know things that no one else knows and you can see things no one else can see, so reflect on your thoughts and you soon will realize things about yourself that only you can discover and things that others assume....(3D)

December 30

Uplift the younger people in your life so they can get even further than you did. They are the ones who will lift our desires to reality. By uplifting them and encouraging their dreams, we allow them to gain all the things that we were unable to accomplish...(3D)

December 31

Plan precise calculated steps toward your goals and things will align to create a path to your destiny. You can't get what you want without knowing how you should get there. You must plan your path carefully and analyze the plan to see where it has flaws. Fix the flaws and correct your plan so your path ends in victory and happiness...(3D)

Questions

1. If you could be nicer to one person in your life who would it be and why?

2. If you could free yourself from one burden in your life what would it be?

3. Who are you?

www.AMileADay.com

3D

Desire + Determination = Dreams

www.ingramcontent.com/pod-product-compliance
Lightning Source LLC
Chambersburg PA
CBHW021229090426
42740CB00006B/453